# MILLER'S Golf MEMORABILIA

To Ivor, David, Daniel and Dionna
Our top collection

Miller's Golf Memorabilia
Sarah Fabian-Baddiel

First published in Great Britain in 1994
by Miller's
an imprint of Reed Consumer Books Limited
Michelin House, 81 Fulham Road
London SW3 6RB
and Auckland, Melbourne, Singapore and Toronto

© 1994 Reed International Books Limited

Series Editor Frances Gertler
Editor James Chambers
Assistant Editor Katie Piper
Art Editor Sue Michniewicz
Production Heather O'Connell
Index Hilary Bird
Special Photography Ian Booth

Contributing Consultants: Duncan Chilcott
Alick Watt (Chapter One: Equipment)

A CIP catalogue record for this book is available from
the British Library

ISBN 1 85732 350 5

Set in Adobe Garamond and Univers Condensed
Origination by Scantrans Pte Ltd, Singapore
Produced by Mandarin Offset
Printed in China

Jacket Illustrations:
(front, clockwise) a silver ball-shaped mustard pot, c.1922; *The Silver
Queen*, a papier-mache promotional figure; a silver and enamel medal,
c.1910; a hickory shafted sand iron, c.1904; an Allan Robertson feather
ball; a poster by Roger Broders advertising a French resort; (back) an
American machine-made golfing pullover by Robert Scott.

# MILLER'S

# Golf

## MEMORABILIA

## Sarah Fabian-Baddiel

# Contents

# Introduction

Golf has been played for many hundreds of years, and in the last two centuries the high profile of the game has meant that it has become a theme for pieces in a number of fields. Such is the popularity of golf that items connected with the game, known as "golfiana", have begun to be collected by enthusiasts. Prices which rose steadily over the past decade have now begun to fall in response to the economic climate, and auctions now have something to offer everyone. It is not only the major sales that are of interest to collectors: second-hand shops and antiques markets can be good places to start, and specialist dealers hold a wide selection of items. The variety of golf memorabilia available serves to show the influence that the game has had over the years.

Some say the origins of golf are to be found in the ancient Roman game *paganica*, in which a club was used to strike a ball stuffed with feathers across the countryside. They say that the Roman legions played it; and if they are right, their theory would certainly explain why, in the Middle Ages, similar games emerged simultaneously in several northern European countries – "jeu de mail" in France, "het kolven" in Holland and "cambuca", "cambrel" or "cammock" in England.

Undoubtedly, however, the Dutch game, usually played on ice, was the one which gave modern golf much of its basic terminology. The word for the game itself, "golf", comes from the Dutch word for a club, "kolf". The pile of sand from which a Dutch player drove off was called a "tuitje" (pronounced toytee). The hole was called a "put", and if anything stood between the ball and the hole, the player said "stuit mij" ("it stops me", pronounced "stytmy").

In the early Middle Ages there were strong trading links between Holland and Scotland, and by the end of the 14th century many Scots were playing a game very similar to the modern one on the long "links" of thin grass and sand which lie along their rugged coast between the solid farmland and the sea. By the end of the 15th century their kings were avid players. Mary, Queen of Scots, played regularly at St. Andrews. When her son James inherited the throne of England, he brought the game south with him to London. James I played on Blackheath common beyond Greenwich; and although the Scots would like to deny it, the society of golfers which was founded there in 1608 was the origin of the world's oldest golf club.

The Royal Burgess Golfing society of Edinburgh is said to have been founded in 1735; and the Company of Gentlemen golfers, now known as the Honourable Company of Edinburgh Golfers, was established in 1744. This company, which recorded the first rules for the game, first played on the Leith links, but later transferred to the famous links at Musselburgh, and then to

Muirfield, where it survives to this day. The most famous club, however, the Royal and Ancient, was formed as the Society of St. Andrews on 14 May 1754. By 1919, when it accepted management of the British Open and Amateur Championships, the Royal and Ancient had become so prominent that it was recognised as the governing body of British golf.

There are a few records of "het kolven" being played in America in the 17th century. In the following century, there was an advertisement for golf clubs in the *Gazette* in New York in 1779 and an announcement of the formation of a club in The *Charleston City Gazette* and *Daily Advertiser* in 1788. But so far as it is known the oldest established golf club on the American continent is the Royal Montreal, which was not established until 1873. In the United States the oldest club is the Foxburg Golf Club in Pennsylvania, which was founded some time before 1887, and the next oldest is probably the St. Andrew's Golf Club of Yonkers, New York, which was named after the great club in Scotland and appropriately took the lead in the forming of the U.S. Golf Association.

The great tradition of craftsmanship in the making of golfing equipment is almost as old as the game itself. In 1603, shortly before he inherited the throne of England, King James VI of Scotland appointed William Mayne as his Royal Clubmaker, and in 1618, as James I of England, he granted a ball-making monopoly to James Melville, who had the right to sell his products for the enormous price of four shillings each. In the centuries that followed, the development of the game was led as much by the craftsmen, particularly the ballmakers, as by the players. With the introduction of each new harder type of ball, for example, the clubmakers developed the larger heavier clubs that could strike them further down the fairway.

As in many other games, the skills of the craftsmen were admired by the players. Old clubs were often kept for display when new designs replaced them on the links. In 1866 a collection was put on permanent display in the Union Club House in St. Andrews, and in 1901 there was a large international exhibition of golf memorabilia in Glasgow.

More recently the boom in golf collecting has been as big as the boom in the game itself which took place almost exactly a hundred years earlier. Few items available to collectors today were made before 1800, however, and those that were are the treasures of any collection, but the field is now so rich and varied, and like golf so infinitely fascinating, that it can offer the satisfaction of a lifetime's hobby to anyone with an enthusiasm for the game. There is nothing connected with golf, no matter how remotely, that is not of interest to at least one group of collectors, and the rare old clubs and balls by the great master craftsmen of the 18th and early 19th century are now as valuable and sought after as works of art.

Sarah Fabian-Baddiel

# Equipment

For the first few hundred years of golf's history, the game was played with leather balls stuffed with feathers and five or six wooden clubs, which the players or their caddies carried loose under their arms. In the 1850s, when the harder gutta percha ball became popular, the wooden clubs became heavier and increased in variety, and they were soon joined by an almost equal variety of the iron clubs which had been popularized by the outstanding play of "Young Tom" Morris of St. Andrews. When Willie Park Jr. won the British Open in 1887, he used five woods and five irons. By the beginning of the 20th century, when the rubber-core precursor of the modern ball was introduced, the range of golfing equipment had increased to a level that was little short of what it is today. There were as yet no trolleys, but the number of clubs used by the average player had grown so much that they were now being carried in a canvas bag, and players were using wooden tees when they drove off instead of making little piles of sand.

By the time the rubber ball was introduced, golf had become so popular that mass production had found its way into a world that had previously belonged entirely to individual craftsmen. Clubs and balls were being made in factories as well as workshops. Most club heads were being shaped by machine tools and only finished off by hand. To cope with the harder balls, harder woods were being used for the heads and even harder inserts were being fitted to their faces. Sockets replaced splicing for the join between shaft and head. In the making of the iron clubs, drop forging soon replaced hand forging, and the lines on the club faces, which added spin to the balls, were put on, not by hand, but by specially designed machines. By the early 1930s even the hickory shafts had been replaced by high-carbon steel.

Some of the clubs that were made quite recently can be of interest to collectors, but there is no doubt that by far the most valuable and sought after prizes – the "Chippendales" of golf equipment – are the earliest long-nosed wooden clubs and the irons that were made by blacksmiths and golf professionals before 1890, par-

ticularly those that can be attributed to the acknowledged masters of their craft.

The appearance of the old wooden clubs can often be improved by a simple clean with a cloth and soapy water. In the same way, an old rusty iron club can be cleaned with oily emery paper. But like any work of art or any piece of antique furniture, an old club will lose much of its value if it is over cleaned or heavily restored. Rust and grime can be removed, although not with anything as powerful as a chemical rust remover or a stripper, but an old club should look old, and both wooden and iron heads should be allowed to retain the patina of age.

Many old clubs will have had their shafts replaced at some time or other, and the leather grip on a replacement shaft, no matter how ragged, will probably be a replacement itself. But these are only the inevitable signs of a long and active life. They do not detract from a club's value in the same way as over-zealous restoration. Unfortunately, however, since most old clubs show signs of later refurbishment, it is all too easy for unscrupulous but skilful dealers to create relics out of reproductions or much more recent clubs. If they have any doubts, always ask for a written guarantee which will entitle the buyer to his or her money back if the club turns out not to be what it was sold as.

*(left, top) Three early canvas golf bags; left to right: £80–120, £100–150, £80–120*
*(left, main) A long-nosed driver made around 1885 by R. Forgan & Son of St. Andrews; £1,000–1,500*
*(above) A feathery golf ball made by one of the great ballmakers John Gourlay; £3,500–5,000*

# Long Nosed Clubs

Before 1880 the design and construction of golf clubs changed very little. Throughout the first 400 years of the game's known history they were made with long, whippy wooden shafts and slim, long-nosed heads, which had a strip of horn inserted along the leading edge of the sole, to prevent wear, and a lead-filled cavity at the back, to give them weight. Very few of the earliest clubs have survived, however. Although there are one or two 18th century clubs on display at St. Andrews and Troon, a collector would be lucky to find anything that was made before 1820.

There between seven to nine basic types of club in an original, "long-nosed" wooden set: a play-club or driver; a grassed driver; a driving putter; three varieties of spoon – long, middle and short – for different distances; a baffing spoon; a niblick; and a putter. First made by specialist craftsmen, in the middle of the 19th century, however, many professional golfers and their families turned to club-making, including the Parks, the Dunns, Morrises and McEwans.

From the early 19th century most makers stamped their names on the heads of their clubs, but these will inevitably be worn. Be wary of marks on old clubs that appear deep, even and relatively unscathed, they may be fakes.

▲ The long-nosed driver, which was used to gain distance from the tee, has a long tapering shaft, which is particularly slender above the spliced joint, and has a thickly padded grip to cushion mis-hit shots.

This excellent example with a thorn head and hickory shaft is stamped McEwan and was made around 1855, possibly by Douglas McEwan, who was the best clubmaker in the family. The famous firm of McEwan was founded by his grandfather James in 1770, and continued through four generations, until the 1880s.

**£2,500 -4,000**

▶ Spoons, or "scrapers" were made for shots on the fairway and differed only in the length of the shaft and the increasing degree of loft. This one, with a beech head and greenheart shaft, was made by Charlie Hunter around 1880. Hunter took over as professional at Prestwick in 1864 when "Old Tom" Morris returned to St. Andrews.

**£2,000-4,000**

◀ The baffing spoon was made with a generous loft and a stiff shaft for baffing, or hitting the ball with maximum lift and minimum run. This is a rare example by Thomas Dunn, the professional at Musselburgh, Wimbledon and several other clubs. He made golf clubs from 1870–1890 and also designed over 130 courses.

**£2,000-3,000**

► The niblick was well lofted and weighted to lift the ball from a bad lie, and this one was made around 1885 by none other than the great Tom Morris, one of the giants of golfing history. "Old Tom" started his clubmaking business in St. Andrews in 1867 after winning the Open for the fourth time.

**£1,000-1,500**

◄ This hickory shafted driving putter, for running low shots, was made around 1870 by Robert Forgan. Forgan took over the St. Andrews business on the death of his uncle Hugh Philp in 1856. After his appointment as clubmaker to the Prince of Wales in 1863, he stamped most of his clubs with the Prince of Wales' feathers. When the Prince became King Edward VII in 1901, Forgan's mark became a crown.

**£800-1,500**

▼ The grassed driver was marginally shorter in both head and length than the driver and had a slight loft to lift the ball down wind. This one, with thorn head and hickory shaft, was made around 1830 by the greatest of all clubmakers, Hugh Philp, who made clubs at St. Andrews between 1810 and 1856 and was so renowned that his clubs were being sought out by collectors within a few years of his death.

**£4,000-6,000**

◄ This modern reproduction of a long-nosed McEwan driver shows the spliced joint between shaft and head characteristic of all long-nosed clubs. When the joint was bound with pitched twine or whipping, a tongue (½ in, 1.2cm) was left exposed at the bottom. On clubs that have been inexpertly re-shafted, the whipping covers the joint completely. The price below applies to a stained and varnished club.

As on most early clubs, the head is made of beech and the shaft of ash. The makers did experiment with many other woods: thorn and most hard fruit-woods were tried on the heads, and whippy hazel was almost as popular as ash for the shafts, but eventually American woods proved to be the most consistently predictable. From the 1840s most shafts were made of hickory, and a growing number of heads from persimmon.

**£100-150**

# *Transitional & Bulger Woods*

When the gutty ball replaced the softer feather ball, in the second half of the 19th century, players and clubmakers soon realised that the elegant long-nosed wooden clubs were no longer strong enough to survive the impact of a shot. In the mid-1880s, in a form that became known as "Transitional", the necks were made thicker and the heads shorter. In 1887, however, and again in 1889, the great Willie Park Jr. won the British Open with a "Bulger" driver, which as the name implies, was made with a rounded bulge on the face. With its supposed greater control over the ball, the bulger, invented by Henry Lamb, soon became a popular wooden club among professionals and low-handicap amateurs.

In the golfing boom of the 1890s, when the number of players multiplied rapidly in both Britain and the United States, the competition for the new custom became fierce and clubmakers continued to experiment with further modifications and new manufacturing techniques. Brass plates were fitted to the bases of wooden drivers, so that they could be swung smoothly without wear on the fairway, and the new clubs became known as "Brassies".

► This transitional driver, made by Robert Simpson of Carnoustie around 1890, is rare and interesting, not only because the rounder-than-usual golden beech head and the hickory shaft are original and in excellent condition, but also because the maker was soon to be one of the pioneers of the "Bulger".

£400-600

◄ Peter Paxton of Musselburgh made both clubs and balls at the end of the last century. This brassie with a beech head and a greenheart shaft, which was made by him around 1890, is in poor condition and has lost its whipping, which shows the spliced joint that was being used in the 1890s.

£200-300

► During the transitional period a few clubmakers experimented with "one piece" clubs. This driver with a leather insert on the face was made from a single piece of hickory around 1905 by the Bridgeport Gun and Implement Company. This already rare example is in unusually fine condition.

£1,500-1,800

▼ The arrival of the rubber core ball led to experiments with aluminium "woods" and a combination of materials. This very rare putter, made by Ray, Sherlock & Turner around 1890 has a sandwich of aluminium, with a socket containing the hickory shaft, and two pieces of persimmon.

£200-300

▲ A good example of a bulger driver, this club was made by Donaldson Bros. around 1922. The curved face with a significantly-reduced striking spot, means that this is not a club for the beginner.

**£150-200**

◄ This is a fine Dunn & Son transitional one piece hickory driver with a sheepskin grip, from around 1900. Although there is a slight crack on the sole, the overall condition is good.

**£1,800-2,200**

▶ As early as 1885, the great master "Old Tom" Morris of St. Andrews was making transitional clubs. This beauty, a brassie, has a beech head and a hickory shaft.

**£800-1,200**

◄ This transitional driver, by an unknown maker but stamped by the London retailers F. & H. Ayres, is more typical of the early transitional shape. Like the Simpson driver, it was made around 1890.

**£250-450**

## COLLECTING

It is important to remember that it is not always necessary to splash out on the oldest and most expensive clubs: there are many other interesting woods that can be bought more reasonably at auction, or better still, at car-boot sales. Clubs worth collecting date up to 1922, and usually have wooden shafts that are in their original form, with no replacement grip for example. Keep a look-out for splice-shafted woods – Harry Vardon was still using one in 1920 – and also socket woods *(see pp.14–15)* with thicker necks and a shorter length of whipping. The most desirable ones are those stamped with the professional's name together with the name of the club that employed him. Interesting pieces include the "Bulldog", a wood with a round, sturdy head; the "Angle shaft" with a "twisted" wooden shaft; and a club stamped "Palakona" with a cane shaft. Never refuse the offer of a wooden club with a champions' name on the head: Vardon, Braid, Taylor, Herd, Cotton and others can all be found at affordable prices, but do make sure they are genuine and in good condition.

# Socket Headed & Through Socket Woods

In the 1890s, when clubmakers were searching for new methods of mass production to meet the rapidly growing demand for their wares, they experimented with new, simplified methods of joining the shafts to the heads, and by the end of the century many were using sockets instead of splicing. The shafts were inserted into sockets on the heads, some about 2in (5cm) in depth, and others going through to the sole. Glued tight and covered in the usual way with whipping, the joins were every bit as effective as splicing and much easier to make. By 1910 socket-head and through-socket clubs had become the most popular, and they remained so until hickory shafts were replaced by steel in the 1920s and 1930s.

There are many more socket clubs on the market than the earlier spliced woods, and they are usually considerably cheaper. In most cases the heads were mass produced and only finished off by the clubmakers and they are occasionally less attractive than the elegant earlier woods. From the 1920s a number of clubs were made with decorative inserts in the faces, using materials such as ivorine, coloured Bakelite and aluminium, which served to prevent wear and tear.

▲ This unusual club is a "bap" head, through-socket spoon, with the usual persimmon head and hickory shaft. It was made around 1912 by D.P. Watt, who was Scottish professional champion in 1914.

**£60-75**

▲ Made around 1918, and still in excellent condition, this socket-head driver by Anderson & Blyth has an unusually small persimmon head. A very straight-faced club, it still has its original shaft and grip.

**£50-75**

► This Mc Gregor driver has a decorative insert in the face made from brown Bakelite held in place by large ivorine pegs.

£45-70

► A steel-shafted Spalding Brassie with a heart-shaped insert. Spalding sponsored Harry Vardon's tour of the United States in 1900. He travelled from coast to coast, and played in a series of exhibition matches, displaying skills that inspired many. That year he won the U.S. Open at Chicago.

£60-80

▲ This putter, made by Robert Simpson of Carnoustie for his exclusive shop in around 1925, has a brass wraparound sole and face, and a "fancy" vulcanite insert fitted with ivorine pegs.

£80-100

▲ Another Spalding Brassie from around 1922, with a coloured insert. Through their sponsorship of Harry Vardon (see above), Spalding were able to put his name to many of their products. For example, a ball known as the "Vardon Flyer" was issued in 1899.

£60-100

◄ A fine example of a rounded-sole "Bulldog" spoon, fitted with a Bakelite insert held by hickory pegs. Made around 1922, this club was ideal for moving the ball from rabbit scapes and "cuppy" lies.

£45-70

# *Orthodox Putters*

As the club that brings success or failure at the end of almost every hole, the putter has always had a special place in the affections of golfers; today the earliest examples are especially popular with club collectors, many of whom specialize in putters alone.

From the outset clubmakers experimented most with the putter: there are more types of putter than there are of any other club. Many are among the more eccentric of the unusual patent clubs, but a number of them are now standard putters which began as patented designs.

A great putter maker, and a man whose clubs are much sought after by both players and collectors was Willie Park, who won the first Open in 1860. He was followed by a long line of makers whose innovations became standard, including his son Willie Jr, who invented the wry-neck putter, George Nicoll, who introduced "The Gem" at the end of the 19th century, and Ben Sayers, who brought out a "Benny" early in the 20th century, with a squared-off handle matching the edges of the blade. The "Benny" was so effective and made such an impact that, when the amended rules of 1984 insisted that the grips on all clubs must be round, an exception was made for putters.

► This long-nosed wooden putter bears the McEwan  stamp. It was made around 1880 by the fourth generation of the great clubmaking family, which moved from Bruntsfield to Musselburgh. Like many putters of its time, it has a beech head with a hardwood insert and a hickory shaft.
**£800-1,200**

◄ Hugh Philp of St. Andrews is thought by many to have been the greatest of all the makers of long-nosed wooden clubs. This elegant putter with a fruitwood head and a hickory shaft was made by him towards the end of his life, around 1850.
**£2,000-4,000**

◄ One of the great champions of golf, "Old Tom" Morris opened his famous club shop at St. Andrews in 1867, and made this beech-headed putter with a hickory shaft around 1885.
Putters designed by the famous man are relatively common and are usually a little less expensive than his other long-nosed clubs.
**£700-1,000**

▶ As an alternative to iron, brass was even more popular on putters than on other clubs. Clubs like this Compass brass putter with the usual hickory shaft from the 1920s are a good start to a collection and are not too difficult to find.

**£45-60**

▶ Willie Park Jr.'s wry neck was copied on many other putters, including this deep-bladed club made around 1925 for Tom Auchterlonie, whose shop in St. Andrews was run by his son until 1992. Auchterlonies, now under new ownership, still flourishes today.

**£70-100**

▼ By the beginning of this century, the most popular iron-headed putters had taken on the shape that is still familiar. This is a Cochrane Castle putter made by Alex Anderson of Anstruther around 1900.

**£50-75**

▶ Sometimes traditionally shaped putters can be made rare and sought after simply by unusual piercing on the face, like the 24 deep holes on this 1920s by William Gibson of Kinghorn, who was then one of the largest clubmakers in the country.

**£100-180**

▼ George Nicoll's patent putter has an elegant curve around the socket and the head. His firm, which began business in 1881, survived in the hands of his descendants until 1982. After 1898, all their clubs, such as this, were stamped with a hand.

**£50-75**

# Unorthodox Putters

In the last century the design of the putter has changed more radically and more frequently than any other club. In the search for perfection, inventors have presented players with often outlandish designs, some of which really did improve their putting, and all of which at least looked as though they might. Some were so successful that they led to protests from the players who were not using them. After Walter Travis, "The Old Man", from the United States won the 1904 British Amateur Championship by putting magnificently with a centre-shafted Schenectady putter, the Royal and Ancient banned the use of centre-shafted clubs in Britain. However, many other successful patents have survived the objections and became so popular that they simply became the prototypes for the next generation's orthodox clubs, and the unsuccessful majority became fascinating relics for which avid putter collectors now scour attics and sale rooms. It is a cycle that seems unlikely to end, and even today experiments continue with ever-more innovative designs. The most popular putter with modern professionals, "the Ping", would certainly have raised eyebrows at St. Andrews in the 19th century.

◀ Slazenger's centre shafted putter had a beautiful hickory head with a heavy, full-length brass inlay on the face. It was made in quite large quantities from 1900 until it became illegal in 1910, and examples are not too difficult to find.

**£250-350**

▶ L. Johnson's rare wooden putter from the 1890s was designed to be used like a croquet mallet and gave the player very little control over the line of the ball. This is exactly the type of well-made curiosity which is highly sought after by collectors.

**£1,500-2,500**

◀ This very unusual centre shafted "Nicola" putter from about 1910 is another that was outlawed by the R. & A. The brass head could be used to strike the ball in three different ways.

**£2,000-3,000**

▼ Not all strange designs were the work of eccentric or unknown designers. This interesting, almost centre-shaft design in the shape of a hoe was brought out around 1900 by the famous R. Forgan & Son of St. Andrews.

**£500-750**

▶ This triangular club, another designed to be swung like a croquet mallet, could be used as a putter on one face and a chipper on the other two. It was made to a patent by Marriott and Ransome in around 1908.

**£300-500**

▼ The holes in a perforated iron might reduce resistance in sand or shallow water, but it is difficult to see what use they would have been on Brown's patent "Perforated Iron" putter. This rare club was only made in the first decade of this century.

**£2,000-3,000**

▶ Made by the prolific manufacturer William Gibson of Kinghorn, the "Jonko" putter with a hump-backed profile like a snail is another comparatively frequent survivor from the 1920s.

**£600-900**

▶ This cylindrical Lloyd Rolling Head Putter, which could never strike the ball cleanly, was patented in 1905.

**£1,000-1,500**

## COLLECTING

While the golf sales of most major British auction houses are held in mid-summer, around the time of the Open Golf Championship, other sales occur more frequently when golfing memorabilia may be sold alongside other sporting collectables. For collectors who live within reach of the auction houses, it is always interesting to view the goods before a sale, whether buying or not, and this is also good way to meet other enthusiasts. It is worth subscribing to one or more auction house catalogues, which are highly illustrated, with comprehensive descriptions of pieces, and estimated prices. They also explain in detail what is involved in selling at, or buying from an auction, and in particular they specify the fees and commission payable to the auction house itself. Finally look out for smaller auctions and sales that may be advertised in the national, county or local press: these may occasionally include a true bargain.

# First Generation Irons

As far as we know iron-headed clubs first appeared at some time in the early to mid-18th century, but it was not until the introduction of the harder gutty ball in 1848 that their use became widespread. Just as the first wooden clubs were made by craftsmen who had learned their skills in some other woodworking trade, the first iron clubs were forged by blacksmiths, many of whom passed them on to have their shafts added by established wooden clubmakers. After 1850, therefore, when iron clubs began to be marked, some carried the names of already famous makers, but there were others that were stamped with the names of the blacksmiths who would later become known, such as John Gray, Alex and Archibald Carrick, R. Brodie, James Anderson, Robert White and Robert Wilson.

This first group of irons consisted of four main types: first, cleeks with a few degrees of loft, for striking the ball as far as possible, and small-headed track irons, for playing out of cart tracks or hoof marks; second, sand irons, mashies and lofters for links courses; and third and fourth, various large-headed, deeply-angled lofters and niblicks, and simple all-purpose irons.

▼ Rut niblicks, with heads larger than track irons but smaller than normal niblicks, were introduced when cart tracks became wider, and they soon became substitutes for sand irons as well. This one was also made by Robert Wilson, around 1880.

Occasionally the heads of rut niblicks are filed down to make them look like the smaller, earlier and more valuable track irons. When buying a track iron collectors should always make sure that there are indentations on the toe of the blade caused by stones and rocks.

**£150-200**

▶ The thick-headed blade on this all-purpose iron was forged around 1895 by Tom Stewart of St. Andrews, to a design by clubmaker James Hutchison of North Berwick, who fitted the hickory shaft. Stewart irons are recognizable by the clay pipe stamped on the head.

**£150-200**

▶ This rare long-faced cleek with an equally long socket on an ash shaft was made by Robert White of St. Andrews around 1880.

In 1890 White emigrated to the United States, where he helped to set up the company that eventually became famous as the McGregor Golf Company.

**£500-600**

▼ This hickory shafted sand iron, forged around 1904, carries the mark of R. Forgan & Son, one of the greatest firms of wooden clubmakers. Like most irons made before 1908, it was originally smooth faced which gave no grip to the ball, but it has been hand punched at a later date.

**£100-150**

▶ Robert Condie of St. Andrews, who was famous for making some of the most beautiful iron heads ever fitted to a wooden shaft, forged this fine lofter for W. Watt of Perth at the beginning of this century.

Condie marked his heads with a rose cleek mark. This is similar to the mark used by the McGregor Golf Company, but it is more upright and there are dots in each petal and a dot in the centre.

**£150-200**

▶ This typical small, but heavy-headed track iron was made for the famous Willie Park of Musselburgh around 1870, by one of the greatest of the early iron clubmakers, Robert Wilson of St. Andrews.

Some of Wilson's clubs were made so early that a few are not marked with his name or a cleek mark, but they are usually easy to recognize as he was the only clubmaker to forge-fuse his heads to the shaft with a bent nail, and the neatly filed ends of the nail show clearly on either side of the hosel.

**£400-600**

◀ A rare and beautifully defined, Robert Forgan autographed jigger. This type of club could be put to many uses with its shallow blade and upright lie. The earliest iron-headed clubs were fashioned by a smith from two pieces of metal: the hosel or socket, and the blade. The process required the maker to be skilled in the use of an anvil, a furnace, and medium- to heavyweight hammers, and at the same time have a knowledge of the game of golf. While the blacksmith found forming the blade of the club a relatively simple task, making the hosel into which the shaft was placed, was much more difficult. Once inserted, the socket was nicked at the top using a hammer and a cold chisel, giving "grip" to the wooden shaft when fitted.

**£80-100**

# Later Iron Clubs

As the popularity of golf increased, blacksmiths and full-time clubmakers began to use machines, such as moulds and mechanical hammers, to turn out their club heads in larger quantities, and they secured the heads more tightly onto the shafts by inserting metal rivets across the sockets. These new craftsmen became known as cleek-makers, after the earliest iron club, and from the 1880s onwards more and more of them followed the example of pioneers like Carrick and Condie who stamped their clubs with identifying "cleek marks" as well as their names. Today there are many collectors who set out to assemble as many as possible of the 150 known cleek marks, rather than full "sets" of clubs by different masters.

After 1895 more iron clubs were introduced and the full set drew closer to the modern numbered series, although they were all still known by individual names – mid- and push-irons, sammys, jiggers, mashies (with varying depths of face), oval-headed mashie niblicks, and putting cleeks. After 1895 some of them had various patterns of hand-punched dots on their faces designed to increase the backspin on the ball, and after 1900, the dots and more recent lined patterns, were applied by machines.

◄ This cleek, still with a straight face as late as 1905, is stamped "Hawkins Never-rust" and is thought to have been made by one of the famous Anderson family, as the sole has the distinctive flange-face. However, the hickory shaft is clearly a clumsy replacement, as, despite the stamp, the rivet has rusted, which it would never have happened on an original.

**£40-50**

► Another fine Anderson club *(see above)*, this time a mashie, with a lined face, a beautifully-shaped flange head and a well polished shaft. Fine clubs like this, made in the second and third decade of this century, are still excellent value for collectors.

**£25-30**

▲ The standard shape of the niblick belies the rarity of the club. Made around 1910, this is possibly one of the last iron-headed clubs to have been made in Musselburgh by the firm of R. Neilson, which was started by his forbears in Leith. "R. Neilson, Musselburgh" is clearly stamped on the back of the blade.

**£80-120**

▲ W. Fulford's rare, shallow-faced, pyramid model push iron, made in 1918, has been skilfully reshafted, using a brass rivet. This is a fine example of a club with the weight behind the ball.

**£50-60**

▲ This fine example of a mid-iron, stamped with the thistle head Albion Brand logo was made around 1912 by George Forrester, who was one of the first to make socket-headed woods and patented an iron club with additional weight behind the "sweet spot". The face of the club is dot marked.

**£50-60**

▲ This oval headed mashie niblick by the King's clubmaker, Robert Forgan & Son, has seen a lot of restoration since it was made in 1905. It has been badly reshafted with a roughly finished rivet and the head has been electroplated. Nevertheless it is essentially a fine club by a great maker and it has value to a collector.

**£60-80**

▶ This large-faced niblick, which first appeared around 1910, inspired a later club, "the mammoth niblick". In keeping with its size and rarity, this one has unusually large, deep punch markings on its face.

**£50-70**

# Aluminium Clubs

Iron, steel and brass are not the only metals that have been used in the manufacture of golf clubs. Towards the end of the last century aluminium was also popular, particularly among the designers of both outlandish and effective patent clubs.

Some of the earliest designers simply produced wooden clubs with heads that had aluminium inserts on the striking face. Others, like Joseph Braddell of Belfast, made aluminium clubs with gutta percha faces. However the great pioneer of the "aluminium wood" was William Mills, who patented a club in 1896 which had an aluminium head with a wooden core. Mills, who was knighted after the First World War, was a leading British industrialist. His works in Sunderland made aluminium cladding for battleships, and he introduced a type of hand-grenade which became known as a "Mills Bomb", but the Standard Golf Company, which made his popular range of aluminium clubs, contributed as much as any other of his interests to his wealth, and continued in production until 1940.

While there are a large number of aluminium-headed clubs around, a great number have cracked hosels or sockets. This is due to inexperienced clubmakers reshafting clubs which have thin, weak metal forming the hosel.

▶ Made by the Standard Golf Company in 1906, this well cared-for and well-balanced putter is stamped "Braid Mills" on the sole, and the date 1906 is stamped on the crown. Together with Harry Vardon and J.H. Taylor, James Braid was one of the great "triumvirate" which dominated British golf at the beginning of the century. Like Taylor, he won the Open five times, while Vardon won on six occasions. As aluminium was usually insufficiently heavy, putters such as this one have a bullet of lead in the back of the club head.

**£90-120**

▼ This very rare double-sided (right- or left- handed) putter was made in 1930 by P.G. David of Clevedon in Somerset, who was one of the largest manufacturers of aluminium tubes for organs.

So that the weight could be adjusted for summer or winter conditions, a brass tube (2in, 5cm) was fitted into the head and held in place with a brass rivet. The end was shut off with a rotating locking screw, and sand or a series of smaller brass tubes could be put inside to increase the weight.

**£750-1,200**

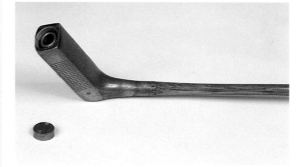

► This long-nosed aluminium putter, fitted with a hickory shaft, was made by William Mills' company, the Standard Golf Company, in Sunderland in 1896. Like most Mills clubs, it has a through shaft, which comes out at the bottom of the club, but, unusually, the face is marked from toe to heel.

**£300-400**

► It looks like a driver, but in fact it is an H. Logan Cherokee Putter made by Gibson of Kinghorn, Scotland. It has an ash shaft fitted on a through socket, and a line indicator on the centre of the head.

These clubs are not rare, but they are nevertheless difficult to find.

**£120-180**

► This rare but unattractive aluminium mashie was made around 1908 by C. & J. Timperley, shafted in hickory by R. Forgan and sold by Mitchells of Manchester. It is for rabbit scrapers, divot marks and short rough.

**£250-500**

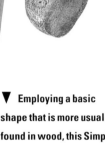

▼ Employing a basic shape that is more usually found in wood, this Simplex type no. 5 iron has a brass insert on the leading edge of the aluminium head. It is stamped A.W. Powell and was made around 1905.

**£800-1,200**

► Another Mills club, this no. 1 cleek made in 1902, has an unusually small head, which looks like a shrunken long-nosed club with a generous loft. This is a great club for seaside links.

**£150-200**

► A very rare club, but also a very well made and well balanced one, This broad-headed, antishank, aluminium putter was made by Joseph Braddell & Son around 1915. The shaft is not on a through socket, and the pattern on the face is very unusual. The only flaw on this club is the rusty rivet.

**£150-200**

# Unusual Metal Clubs

Although the shapes and lengths of iron clubs varied very little over the years, there were many inventors who added to the interest of the game by introducing curious and bizarre shapes designed to improve the success of the player. Not usually favoured by the major manufacturers, most of them were hand made by craftsmen from smaller companies and are now extremely rare. Special features that required particular attention meant that these clubs were generally not suitable for the production line. But out of several hundred patents there were a few clubs which found sufficient favour with players to be mass produced and sold in commercial quantities until they were eclipsed by the arrival of the matched and graded sets which provide the standards for golf clubs today.

Whether rare or commonplace, all unusual metal clubs are sought after by collectors keen to own a golfing oddity and a piece of the game's history, even though very few will command the same sort of prices and respect as the handiwork of the first great clubmakers.

▲ The spring faced iron was an unusually small, through-socket club with an additional face. This 1905 example by Spalding has a fairly upright lie and a shortened shaft, which makes it resemble a jigger of the same period.

Clubs such as this are highly sought after and very rare, as it took a great deal of time to rivet on the striking plate.

**£300-350**

▼ The "Urquhart Adjustable Iron" was made in Edinburgh by the Urquhart family in the late 1890s. The blade of the club rotated at the base of the socket and was adjusted by a cog ratchet, which could be locked. The shape of the blade made the club more comfortable for a left-handed player than a right hander, and there was a disconcerting noise when the ball left the club face. On the whole, the club was more use for practice than for competitive play.

**£600-900**

◀ Another common curiosity from the 1890s is the crescent-headed iron, in this case a driving iron, made by Anderson of Edinburgh. The club was difficult to use – if the head bit too deep into the ground, the ball came off the shaft – but the rounded sole was useful for extricating the ball from rabbit scrapes and hoof marks.

**£500-900**

◄ The most common and widely used of the unusual patent clubs were the anti-shank irons. This one was forged around 1912 by Anderson of Anstruther to the patented design of F.G. Smith. The reverse of the blade has a special toe and heel weighting at the end.

**£85-120**

► Beside Smith, the other leading designer of anti shank irons was F. Fairlie. This, the first of his designs, has a face ahead of the shaft. It was forged by Tom Stewart of St. Andrews around 1915.

**£85-120**

► The mammoth niblick was made for hitting a ball out of the deepest bunkers, particularly when it was trapped inside a footprint, but it was also good for use in dense rough, as the large thin blade cut through most of the weeds and scrub in its path. The club was always very cumbersome and often marked the wooden-headed clubs when it was removed from the bag. This one was made by Ben Sayers around 1920.

**£400-600**

► Another "must" for the collector of unusual clubs is the rake iron, designed to be used in sand or water. Like the mammoth niblick, it usually damaged the wooden clubs if it was not returned with extra care to the bag. This one, to the design of Brown's Patent Perforated Niblick, was made by Winton & Co. of Montrose around 1906.

**£2,500-3,500**

## FAKES

Even in present times a few "unique" clubs are still being made to look like antiques. Skilled crafstmen can easily bend or twist the socket or blade of an old iron or putter and sell it as a golfing curiosity at a vastly inflated price. Should such a piece be offered to you, before buying inquire about its history and past owners, and ask for a receipt of payment. This is a reasonably expensive area of collecting, so be sure not to be duped by unscrupulous dealers.

## COLLECTING

When collecting clubs it is important to learn the best ways to look after and display them. Keeping a club in good condition and storing it carefully will extend its life, and may even help to increase its value in the long run. With this in mind, it may be a good idea to find an insurance company that will provide realistic cover for your collection.

# Feather Balls

For the first 400 years, golf was played with a leather-covered ball stuffed with feathers. Making a "feathery" was a slow and skilful process, and few ball makers could produce more than four in a day. The leather was first softened with alum and water and then cut into three or four pieces. These were sewn together with waxed thread leaving a small gap prior to turning the skin inside out – an operation not without difficulty – so that the seams were on the inside. Then the maker crammed the little orb with boiled goose feathers, using a crutch-handled steel stuffing rod. When the wet ball dried, the feathers expanded and the leather contracted, making it tight and hard enough to be hit over long distances.

Before the 1820s very few makers stamped their names on their balls, but after that the practice became increasingly common, and in most cases the names of the best early 19th century ball makers can still be seen on their surviving handiwork, among them the Gourlays, Tom Morris, Thomas Alexander and the greatest of them all, Allan Robertson.

Collectors are unlikely to find genuine feather balls anywhere other than in sale rooms or dealers' shops. There are now a few fakes around, which are usually too soft and do not look sufficiently old.

◄ David Marshall of Leith was another of the leading early 19th century ball makers. This one, in good condition, is 1¾ in (4.5cm) in diameter.

£2,500-3,500

► Rarity can make a ball valuable, even when it is in very poor condition. This well-used feather ball from around 1850 is still worth well over £1,000.

£1,500-2,500

◄ The seams are intact, but otherwise this mid-19th century ball, 1¼ in (3cm) in diameter, is in poor condition and has been well used.

£1,500-2,000

► Made around 1845 and measuring approximately 1⅝ in (4cm) in diameter, this is one of the last generation of feather balls and weighs around 1½ oz (42.5g).

£2,200-2,800

► This beautiful feather ball in excellent condition was made by one of the masters of the craft, John Gourlay of Musselburgh, around 1835. Balls made by Gourlay consistently fetch large amounts at auction, and as skilled ballmakers could make only a few featherics in a day, they were relatively expensive, even at the time.

**£4.000-5,000**

◄ This early 19th century ball by an unknown maker is a little larger than most with a diameter of 1⅞ in (4.5cm). The seams are splitting and the leather is slightly cracked, but it is still a highly sought-after treasure.

**£2,000-3,000**

► Made by Thomas Alexander of Mussel-burgh, another master, around 1830, this feather ball in good condition has a diameter of 1⅝ in (4.2cm). The final stitching is visible above and below the seam.

**£6,000-8,000**

◄ The greatest maker of "featheries", Allan Robertson (see right), simply marked his balls "Allan". This one (1⅝ in, 4.2cm) features the number 29 together with the owner's initials. Although slightly out of shape, this is one of the greatest prizes of the golf collecting world.

**£10,000-14,000**

## COLLECTING

While most feather golf balls were made up of three lobes of leather, other balls with outer skins – usually goatskin – and, feather filled may be offered as "featheries". These have a "petal" shape with four lobes, and these are in fact ball made for the game of "fives" and not golf. The stitching of a fives ball is on the outside of the skin, and is usually made of thin wire rather than thread: it is impor-tant to be aware of this intruder.

## ALLAN ROBERTSON

Allan Robertson came from a ball-making family which had been in trade at St. Andrews for many generations, and Allan's father David, was the agent for Peter McEwan's famous clubs. Born in 1815, Allan was the one of the best players of his time. Against his contemporaries, the Dunn twins and Old Tom Morris, Robertson played many great matches and helped to establish the pre-eminence of St. Andrews as a golfing centre. He died in 1859 aged 40, and sadly never had the chance to win the title of Open Champion, a tour-nament established in 1860.

# Gutta Percha Balls

In 1848 a new, less expensive type of golf ball was introduced. The ball was made of gutta percha, a substance like rubber but harder and less elastic, which was being imported into Britain from its Indian and Malaysian empire. Surprisingly, however, nobody knows for certain who invented it. Many believe that it was invented by Robert Paterson, who moulded balls out of the gutta percha that had been used to pad a statue sent from Singapore, but there are others who believe that the inventor was William Smith, a clockmaker from Musselburgh.

The "gutty ball" as it became known, was made from moulded strips of gutta percha. One of its advantages was that it could be melted and re-moulded when it had been knocked out of shape. It could also be cut and marked, which was not initially recognised as an advantage, but when caddies started to play with lost or discarded balls which had been disfigured by slicing, they discovered that the aerodynamic effect of the cuts improved the flight of the ball. By the mid-1850s most of the ball makers were hand-hammering the surfaces of their balls with random indentations, and in about 1860 Robert Forgan began to mark his balls with a criss-cross pattern. Moulds were introduced in the 1860s.

◄ Although it has been well used, this early example of a hand-hammered gutty ball still retains some of its paint, and it has been marked in the style that was introduced by Robert Forgan. Balls like this give collectors a chance to exercise their own judgement and decide whether or not they are buying a bargain. It is possible that this ball was made by Forgan.

**£500-600**

► The moulded "bramble pattern" became extremely popular in the 1890s, as on this "Cormorant" by G. Breeze.

**£300-400**

▲ The smooth gutty balls, which were only made between 1848 and the mid-1850s are much the rarest and on the whole the most expensive, although one in average condition, like this one by an unknown maker, can be a very good investment.

**£1,500-2,000**

▼ The rarest balls of any type are those that were painted red instead of white for use in snow. Rarest of all are the smooth red guttys, which can be very valuable even when they only retain traces of their paint.

**£2,000-3,000**

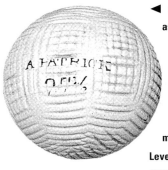

◀ Although not as scarce as the smooth balls, hand-hammered guttys are much rarer than those with moulded patterns. This one, in fine, unused condition, was made by Alex Patrick of Leven around 1865.

**£1,000-2,000**

▲ The mesh or lattice pattern was perhaps the most popular of all on gutty balls. This one was made in Musselburgh around 1860.

**£450-500**

▶ Red paint was being used on golf balls in the 1880s, and some makers, like Archie Simpson, were applying it rather appropriately to "bramble pattern" balls.

**£450-500**

## COLLECTING

As gutty balls were prone to cracking if not laid aside to season for six months after they were made, it is important to check for signs of cracking when considering a purchase. If a ball shows signs of cracking it is fairly certain that this will become worse unless the ball is stored somewhere cool, dry and away from direct sunlight. When handling, avoid pressure from the thumb and forefinger, and this will also extend the life of the ball.

▼ In the last decade of the 19th century, some ballmakers were producing balls in a mixture of gutta percha and rubber. Many have survived in quite good condition and they are among the least expensive of the 19th century balls.

**£100 each**

# *Rubber Core Balls*

The third great step forward in the development of the modern golf ball, which came in 1898, was also the first great step to come from the United States. In that year Coburn Haskell and Bertram Work of Akron, Ohio, applied for a patent to make a ball with a gutta percha cover and a centre composed of elastic rubber thread wound round itself under tension. They received their patent in the following year, and in 1900 the engineer whom they had employed to make the balls, John Gammeter, obtained a patent for a thread-winding machine.

These new "Haskell balls" were not at first a success. Although they could travel a great distance, even when they had not been struck properly, they were difficult to control and were nicknamed "Bounding Billies". In fact, the problem was solved by accident. Thinking he was remoulding a gutty ball, the professional at the Chicago Golf Club, James Foulis, inadvertently remoulded a Haskell in a bramble pattern mould, instead of the mesh pattern which all Haskells had used until then. The resulting ball was easily controlled. In 1902 Sandy Herd won the British Open with a Haskell. By 1910, rubber core balls had replaced the guttys as the most popular in the world.

▲ A.G. Spalding & Bros. one of the largest of all ball manufacturers, was also one of the first to obtain a licence to make rubber core balls. This one, the Spalding 50, was brought out in 1919.
**£80-120**

▲ This rare early rubber core ball features a mesh pattern, but it is unusual because the moulding is extremely small.
**£300-400**

◄ Rarest of all, this early DIO 1 rubber core ball has been marked with concentric rings instead of a mesh. If the ball were not in such distressed condition, it would be more valuable than the ball with the miniature mesh pattern *(see above)*.
**£150-250**

▲ Made before 1905, this early rubber core ball has a mesh pattern that is slightly smaller than usual.

**£150-200**

▲ Collectors are not usually interested in more recent golf balls, but there are some balls which are rare exceptions, among them the signed balls which presidents of the United States have had made as souvenirs for their golfing partners and opponents.

**£100-150**

▼ Spalding's most popular ball, the Kro-Flite, was made with a mesh surface in 1920, and a dimple pattern, originally developed by William Taylor in 1905, seen here, in 1922. The dimple or recessed cover was thinner than the mesh.

**£80-120**

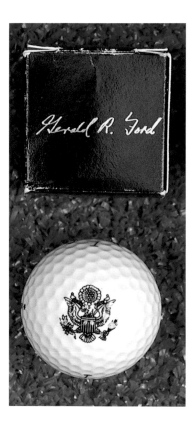

◄ As well as featuring a signature *(see above)*, a presidential golf ball is marked with the arms of the United States. Presidential balls are made with individual presentation boxes, also featuring the leader's signature.

**£100-150**

# *Ball Boxes*

Apart from being sold separately, golf balls have always been sold in boxes of three, six or a dozen. Many people collect the boxes for their own sake, but to all box and ball collectors the rarest treasure of all is a complete set of a dozen old unused balls still wrapped and in their box. Open ball boxes make a colourful display and they are an excellent way of tracing the history and development of the ball.

The companies who produced the greatest variety of balls and whose striking boxes are the most sought after by collectors are The North British Rubber Co. of Edinburgh, the Silvertown Co. of London, Slazenger & Sons of New York and London, A.G. Spalding & Bros, the St. Mungo Manufacturing Co. of Newark, New Jersey and Glasgow, particularly its many "Colonel" balls, the Dunlop Tyre & Rubber Co. of Birmingham and New York, and the Worthington Rubber Co. of Elyria, Ohio.

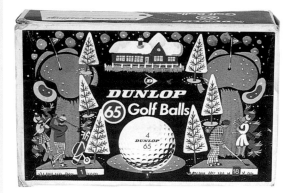

▲ A much more recent product, almost too recent to be of interest to the serious collector, this box of six Dunlop 65s from the 1960s is rare and collectable because it is still in its Christmas wrapper.

**£20-40**

▼ Although the firm had been operating since the beginning of the century, St. Mungo first made its famous "Colonel" balls in 1909. This tin once contained a dozen balls, but it is still a valuable and evocative collectors' item on its own.

**£120-200**

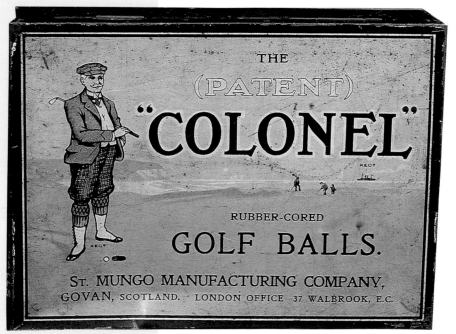

▲ J.B. Halley of London introduced Ocobo gutty balls in 1894, following them with a rubber core version in 1914. Again it is rare to find a full box of such old balls unused and in their original tissue paper.

**£700-1,100**

◄ Michelin was another great rubber and tyre company that turned to making golf balls. This simple and attractive triangular box of six, three of which are still in their wrappers, was made around 1935.

**£200-300**

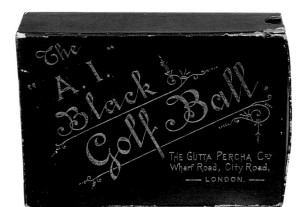

◄ Marketing gimmicks were not unknown even in the 1890s. The A1, which was produced by the Gutta Percha Co. in London in 1894, was also sold in red.

**£50-70 box only**

▼ This is a very rare find indeed, a box of a dozen unused Spalding Bramble Gutty Balls made around 1897. These are some of the first balls made by the company and the first to be stamped with the Spalding name.

**£5,000-6,000**

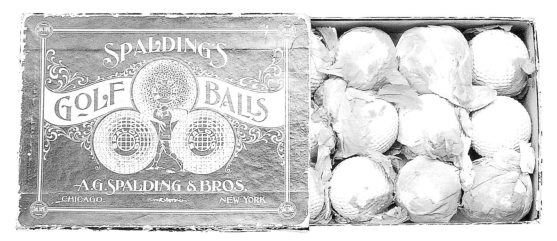

# Ball Moulds

One of the great advantages of the gutta percha ball was that it could be re-moulded after it had become chipped and misshapen through use. Most professionals allowed their customers to trade in old balls in part payment for new ones and then sent the old ones back to the manufacturers to be re-modelled. But by the end of the 19th century a growing number of amateur golfers were buying one of the many moulds on the market and restoring their balls themselves.

After removing the paint with a stripper, the golfers heated their balls in a pot of almost boiling water. Once the balls had become soft, they took them out one by one with a spoon, rolled them between their palms to smooth out all the cuts, and then, after squeezing them into an egg shape, pressed them tightly for about a minute between the two halves of the mould. After that the balls were dropped into cold water to cool off quickly in their good-as-new shape and then repainted.

Several companies sold special presses and sets of moulds in different sizes with different patterns on them, but many golfers simply bought the moulds by themselves and pressed the two halves together with book presses or weights.

▲ John White & Co.'s cast-iron press was neater and slightly smaller than most. This one, from around 1900, comes complete with a mould for a square mesh ball.
**£3,000-4,000**

◀ The presses made by G. Brodie Breeze of Glasgow were more substantial than the John White models. This one, also made around 1900, has a mould for a mesh pattern ball.
**£2,500-3,500**

The Breeze moulds were almost urn shaped and were made of cast iron rather than brass. This one, from the same period as the press and made for a size 26½, square mesh patterned ball, is typical of Breeze's products, although it carries no maker's stamp. It was probably originally part of a set that accompanied a press.

£500-700

▼ Most ball moulds show the wear and staining caused by use. This example is exactly the same model as in the previous illustration, a John White & Co. mould for a square mesh ball size 27, but, even though it was made at least 20 years later, around 1920, it has clearly been used a great deal.

£350-450

▼ John White & Co. of Edinburgh, who were essentially brass founders and plumbers, were among the leading manu-facturers of ball moulds. This brass mould for a square mesh, size 27 ball was made around 1895. Although there is no short-age of moulds like this on the market, this one is unusual because it is in perfect condition.

£600-1,000

▶ Many ball moulds from the turn of the centu-ry do not have a maker's mark on them. This cast iron example, from about 1895, is rather larger and heavier than most.

£500-700

▲ The rarest moulds are those that have ingenious mechanisms for clamping the two halves together, but this does not usually make them any more expensive. This one, also unmarked, was made around 1905.

£500-700

▲ John White & Co. also made moulds for the other patterned balls. This one, in quite good condition, made around 1917, was for the "Trophy" dimple pattern ball.

£500-700

# Golf Bags

Before the last quarter of the 19th century, golfers or their caddies simply carried their clubs under one arm. In those days most serious golfers played with between 8 and 15 clubs, but when the first realistic club carrier came along, it was designed to take no more than 6, balanced on a strip of wood between two handles.

In the 1890s, however, manufacturers introduced wicker carrying tubes and patented tripod bags known as "Golf Caddies", which could hold up to 10 clubs. Then, at the beginning of the 20th century, canvas bags reinforced with leather, with handles and shoulder straps were introduced. These varied in size to carry between 6 and 10 clubs, but as more clubs became necessary, bags grew larger and steel supports were added to prevent them from sagging, and in the 1920s, when zip fasteners replaced buckles, the number of pockets on the bag increased.

Early tripod "caddies" and bags made from army surplus webbing in the 1920s highly collectable, but all bags made before the Second World War are collected, and in good condition they are all relatively valuable.

▼ By the end of the 1930s golf bags had taken on the shape that remains familiar today. This one in coloured canvas and leather, made for Lillywhites in 1938 by Jabez Cliff of Walsall, will hold 14 clubs and accessories.

**£100-150**

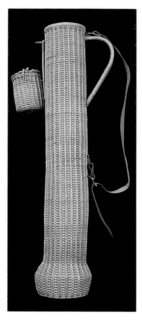

▲ The design of the wicker tube club carrier changed very little between the 1890s and the 1900. This one, in very good condition, was made by an unknown manufacturer.

**£300-700**

◄ The other leading manufacturer at the end of the last century was George G. Bussey & Co. of Queen Victoria Street, London. Bussey's "Stand Up" caddy was very similar to Osmond's, but it was slightly taller, almost always had three wooden legs, and usually had two smaller handles or a single handle like this one, which was made around 1900. To add to the confusion, however, some of the later "Automatons" *(see facing page)* were also made with this style of handle. Bussey's products command the same prices as Osmond's, but this one is only in fair condition.

**£400-800**

▼ Osmond's Automaton was popular for several decades and was made under licence by several other manufacturers. This one, with three wooden legs, was made in the 1920s by John Jacques & Son.

**£700-1,100**

▲ One of the two companies that dominated the manufacture of patented "caddies" in the 1890s was Osmond's of Lee Green, London, which produced the "Automaton". The contraption had two steel legs and one larger wooden leg with an adjustable canvas holder at the bottom, a ball bag at the top and two large curved leather handles.

**£700-1,400**

◄ Most of the bags produced in the 1930s provided more space for balls, clothes and other equipment, and many, like this one in canvas and leather, had the first hoods which were fastened to the side to use as pockets. It was made in 1934 by J. Bryant Ltd. of Kennington, London.

**£90-180**

► From 1900 until the end of the 1920s the basic shape of leather and canvas bags was very similar to the simple tube design of wicker carriers. This one in machine stitched calf skin has the usual steel ring supports, aluminium inside the base for strength, and strong studs on the outside to protect the leather from wear on the grass.

In order to preserve the leather, old bags like this should occasionally be rubbed with saddle soap.

**£200-300**

◄ Golf bags are among the few articles for which golf enthusiasts are not prepared to pay more than collectors of luggage in general because condition, age and style are all-important. This one, however, would be keenly sought by both sorts of collector as it was made in Paris in the 1930s by Hermès. A company that was established at the time as one of Europe's leading makers of saddles and harnesses, Hermès is now one of the most fashionable companies in the world.

**£250-350**

# *Tees*

In the early 19th century, when the teeing ground for one hole was just part of the green on the previous hole, boxes of sand were deposited at the sides of the greens, so that players could make little piles from which to drive off their balls. At some of the better clubs the caddies carried their own leather bags of damp sand, which could be shaped more easily into roughly the same height each time, and by the 1890s most keen players were using tee moulds, which made the little damp mounds exactly the same height. By 1900, however, wooden tees in the modern shape had been introduced. These were sold in many different colours, and at first most players always used the same colour, so that they could identify their own tee easily, but once the faces of most wooden clubs had been fitted with harder inserts, the wooden tees broke too easily, and the new plastic tees that were introduced instead cost so little that few players cared if they lost them.

Other types of tee which were popular at the turn of the century were paper cones, cardboard rings and rubber "double-deckers", which could be swivelled to a high or low position.

◀ ▲ Cashing in on the fame of "The Colonel" products, the Virginia Snow Studio of Elgin, Illinois, called its simple cardboard ring tees "Colonel Bogey's". The box contained a dozen.
**£20-60**

◀ On the whole, serious collectors are interested only in full boxes or packs of unused tees. This box of two dozen folded paper tees was sold at the beginning of this century by the St. Mungo Company of Newark, New Jersey and Glasgow, which also manufactured the famous "Colonel" brand of ball.
**£140-180**

▼ Sets of plastic tees introduced in the 1930s had shoulders on their shanks so that they could be set at different heights: long for driving, short for iron shots.

**£4-8 each**

► The early "flat cap" tees made before the first world war had the shape that is familiar today. At the beginning of the century, they were sold for a shilling a hundred.

**£3-6 for a dozen**

▼ These simple wooden tees introduced in the 1920s were known as "carrot tees". They were less likely to break than the tees with slender shanks.

**£3-6 for a dozen**

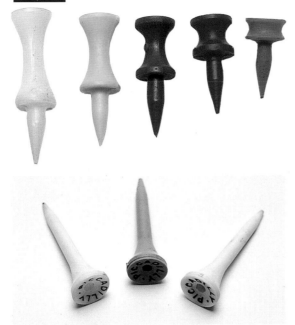

▲ In the 1920s the Wimo Specialty Company of Hudson Falls, New York, patented tees which contained lead inserts to be used as pencils, sold in boxes printed with score cards. The idea was later used on advertising tees issued to competitors at the Piccadilly Tournament, now sponsored by Toyota.

**£8-12 for a dozen**

◄ In the 1920s and 1930s rubber tees were sold for use on hard ground in winter time. They simply sat on the ground, but they were sometimes attached by a cord to steel pins, which could be driven easily into the hard earth, and they had bright tassels, making them quick to find if they flew.

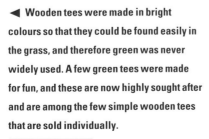

◄ Wooden tees were made in bright colours so that they could be found easily in the grass, and therefore green was never widely used. A few green tees were made for fun, and these are now highly sought after and are among the few simple wooden tees that are sold individually.

**£5-8 for a dozen**

**£4-7**

# Umbrellas & Walking Sticks

At the end of the last century, when it was usual for gentlemen to carry walking sticks, many golfers carried sticks that were shaped like clubs. The best of these were actually rather more than imitations, as they had started out as the "apprentice piece" clubs which were made as part of their training by the club makers' apprentices, and they had then been turned into walking sticks with the addition of more appropriate tapering shafts. The shafts were occasionally made out of English ash or beech, but most of them were made of hickory imported from the United States. At a time when the playing of games on the Sabbath was still frowned upon, these sticks became known as "Sunday Clubs" and were used for surreptitious practice swings during innocent Sunday afternoon strolls.

Not to be outdone by these elegant and useful accessories, the ladies acquired ornate and often extremely expensive parasols and umbrellas with club-shaped handles made out of ivory, silver and gold.

► At first glance this is a comparatively ordinary walking stick made around 1910 with a stained hickory shaft and a rustless iron head shaped like a putter. However, the head is stamped "Forrester, Elie, Earls Ferry" and it also has the initials B. & S.A. in a triangle. George Forrester, who worked in Elie until his death in 1930 is said to have been the first club maker to mount socket-headed woods, in the 1890s, and he also patented the "concentric iron", to which he had added extra weight behind the sweet spot. The initials in the triangle may be those of apprentices or separate manufacturers.

**£160-240**

◄ This hazel stick with silver mounts has a most unusual silver club head with a small cigarette case and match compartment hidden inside it. The value is increased by the engravings: the head is engraved "Allys" and the silver shield on the shaft reads "Whitchurch Golf Club, Presented to Lady Cory, 12.5.23". Lady Cory was the wife of the MP for Whitchurch and was later awarded the CBE.

**£250-400**

▲ A silver golf ball crowns the head of this fine beech-shafted golfing umbrella, made around 1900. At a pull on the strap, a hidden silver-topped pencil pops out from the centre of the ball.

**£150-295**

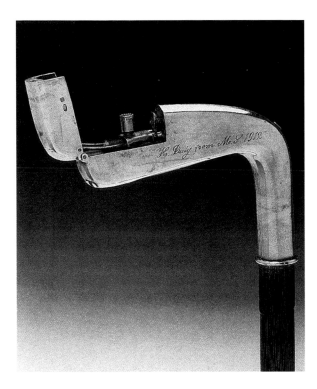

◀ This unusual silver-headed malacca walking stick with a brass ferule was made in Europe and hallmarked in Birmingham in 1911. With a lighter inside the club-head handle, it is attractive not only to golf collectors but also to collectors of smoking memorabilia, which always inflates the price. Another variation of this stick unscrews at the head to reveal a miniature spirit flask inside!

**£400-600**

▼ A good example of a hickory shafted "Sunday stick", this one has a scared, ebonized head with horn insert which has been shaped like an old long nose club. The whipping is still intact, it has a good quality brass ferule and is stamped with a maker's name, G. Brown.

**£200-400**

▼ A brass mesh-patterned ball forms the knob of this fine cane, made in 1888. Rarity and age alone make this a valuable piece, but there is also an important inscription, which reads "Presented to Charles Hunter by the Ladies' Golf Club, Prestwick". Hunter followed Tom Morris as professional at Prestwick. Although he went to Royal Blackheath in 1865, he returned to Prestwick three years later and remained there until his death in 1921.

**£400-650**

▼ Ivory headed walking sticks are rare and highly sought after. This cane has a silver mount and an ivory handle shaped like an old-fashioned long-nose putter.

**£160-300**

◀ Too good to be used as a "Sunday stick", this one was made around 1910, possibly in the U.S.A. The shaft is hickory and the socket head is persimmon with coloured ivory inserts.

**£100-120**

# Clothes & Accessories

Most of the first golf courses were laid out over common land, which was primarily used for grazing cattle and was usually traversed by at least one road. As a result, to make themselves quickly and easily identifiable, the golfers of the mid-18th century wore red coats, similar in colour to the "pink" coats that later became popular on the hunting field. Early versions such as the one worn by "The Blackheath Golfer", were decorated with gold lace and braid and had heavy epaulettes. By the end of the century, the cut had become simpler and more familiar.

Purpose-built courses began to appear at the end of the 19th century, and as there was no longer any need for players to make their presence obvious, men's golfing attire became similar to that worn for shooting. By 1910 red coats were hardly seen anywhere outside the oldest courses, and teams from the oldest universities. But the popularity of golf among the wealthy brought the game to the attention of tailors, designers and the manufacturers of fashion accessories. Throughout this century golfing fashions have changed regularly, echoing other fashions in brighter colours, and the result is another rich field for collectors of golfing memorabilia.

▲ The scarf manufacturing firm of Thirkell came to prominence making propaganda scarves during the Second World War. On this rare example of the firm's post war work, the scenery, and the attire of the Blackheath Golfer and his caddy have been adapted to fit a more traditional Scottish setting. Without its golfing theme, the scarf would be worth considerably less.

**£50-80**

▼ This colour plate comes from a travelling saleman's sample book for tweeds and suit material. Many golf clubs are now

celebrating their centenaries and members have become interested in period clothing as a way of learning more about the history of the game. Pictures such as these are a valuable source of information.

**£70-130**

▶ This attractive unsigned painting from around 1925, features a stylized, Art Deco view of women's golf in the decade. In fact, by this time competitive ladies' golf was firmly established.

**£100-150**

◀ Another example of American golfing fashions, this colour plate also from a sample book *(see left)*, measuring 12x 16in (30.5 x 40.5cm), was produced in around 1910.

**£80-130**

▲ This red playing coat with traditional blue serge cuffs and collar was made for a member of the Cambridge University Golf Club around 1890. These coats are the most sought after of all golfing clothes.

**£300-600**

▼ Demonstrating how the golfing theme was adopted by manufacturers of accessories, this beautifully-made leather handbag from around 1910 features an E.P.N.S clasp shaped like a driver running along the top.

**£90-150**

▶ This painting by J.V. McFall shows how a female golfer would have dressed in 1905. The fitted blouse and long skirt do not give her much room to manoeuvre!

**£200-300**

5¢ a copy
10 Cents in Canada
July 21, 1923

Collier's WEEKLY

SHANKS'S Mowers & Rollers for Golf Courses
1926

# Ephemera

Golf has a long history. The first known reference to the game under this name appears in the records of the parliament held by the King of Scots, James II, in 1457, in which he decreed that football and golf should be banned because they prevented his soldiers from practising archery. It was not until almost 300 years later that the first book entirely devoted to the game was published, and even then it was only a 28-page comic poem, *The Goff*, by Thomas Mattison. But after that the stream of publications continued steadily and grew slowly, until it suddenly spread out in the great golfing boom at the end of the 19th century.

By the beginning of the 20th century, magazines had been established, golfing authors were eagerly meeting the demands of a growing market with a wide

Edna Crompton—

*In this issue:*

46 **They Call It Ruin** *by Richard Washburn Child*

variety of books, not just histories of the game and instruction manuals, but biographies and books about courses and even novels, and the influence of their sport had expanded into almost every area of print – postcards, greetings cards, stamps, and every conceivable kind of packaging and advertising.

The popularity and influence of the game have continued ever since. When a former editor of *Punch*, Alan Coren, recently published a book of comic essays at Christmas time, he conducted some research to find out which were the most popular subjects with the buyers of presents and then named his book accordingly, *Golfing for Cats*, even though there was not a word about either between the covers.

After clubs, books are the richest and most popular field for collectors of golfing memorabilia, but for those with smaller budgets, magazines can be equally rewarding. With their stories of great contemporary tournaments and their articles about the introduction of novel equipment, some of which has long been forgotten and some of which has since become standard. Early editions of the oldest magazines, such as *Golf*, which first appeared in 1890, are a rich source of golfing history.

Postcards are another rich field for collectors on limited budgets. The huge range published in the first few decades of this century provides an opportunity to assemble specialist collections dedicated to the histories of famous courses or tournaments. The cards can be kept in special albums or framed in groups, but the collector should always make sure that framed cards are placed on an acid-free backing.

At some time or another the art directors and advertisers in almost every magazine, no matter what its subject, have used golf as a theme for the illustration on the cover, and these, like the illustrations from old calendars, can be framed to make lively but inexpensive decorations for the walls of a golfer's study or den. As with cards, however, their backing should always be acid-free.

To all collectors, the present is as interesting as the past. Today's books, cards, advertisements and magazines are bound to be tomorrow's collectables, and many modern collectors buy several copies of the best examples – one to read or display, one to bring their collection up to date, and a few more for investment.

*(left, above) Shanks Manfacturer's catalogue for 1926; £18–25*
*(left, main) Cover of Colliers, an American magazine, 1923; £25–40*
*(above) First day covers commemorating Bobby Jones, 1981; £15–30 each*

# *Books*

Books were among the earliest golfing items to attract collectors. By the early 1900s, bibliographers were already compiling lists. The best bibliography is *The Library of Golf*, 1743–1966, by J.S.F. Murdoch, which was published in hardback in 1968 and was followed by an updated card-covered edition in 1978. Today this book is itself a much sought-after collectors' item, although at first it did not sell well, priced at £8. Today however, when a copy can be found, it sells for between £200 and £300.

Almost every golfer has been given a golf book as a gift, and this is often the beginning of a collection. But not all golf books are collectable. Although the best club histories and instruction manuals are highly prized, many are ill-written, parochial and carelessly printed and are consequently of no interest to collectors.

Many of the earliest collectors' classics were first published in limited luxury editions and were often signed by their authors. As these were rare to start with and are even rarer now, they have for a long time been beyond the reach of most collectors, but some of them have since been reprinted, also in limited editions, and in most cases these new editions have become highly collectable in their own right. (The books that might form the basis of a collector's library are marked with their values at the end of the book.)

▶ The dozen or so survivors from the three 18th century editions of the first known golfing book *The Goff* are the most highly prized trophies among collectors of golf books. after the success of the first edition in 1743, a second printing took place in 1763 and then another in 1793. This one is from the third printing, as its date reveals, although it is described as a "second edition".

After 1793 the book was not reprinted until 1981, when it was published by the U.S.G.A.

**£14,000-20,000**

```
                    THE
        G O F F.
              AN
    HEROI-COMICAL POEM.
            IN
        THREE CANTOS.
       SECOND EDITION.

           WITH AN
        APPENDIX;
          CONTAINING
   TWO POEMS IN PRAISE OF GOFF, AND A FEW
       NOTES AND ILLUSTRATIONS.

   Cætera, quæ vacuas tenuissent carmina mentes,
   Omnia jam vulgata.——VIRG.

         EDINBURGH:
   PRINTED FOR PETER HILL.
           1793.
```

▼ The first golfing book to be published in a special limited edition was Robert Clark's *Golf, a Royal and Ancient Game*, which came out in 1875 in a large paper edition of only 50 copies, with each initialled by the author. At a tenth of the price, this ordinary edition went on sale at the same time.

**£275-400**

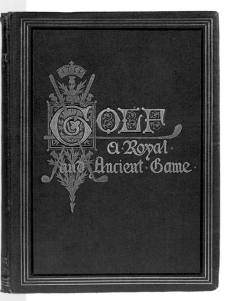

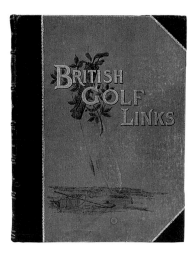

◀ Horace Hutchinson's *British Golf Links* was first published in an unsigned limited edition of 250 in 1897. This copy, a little less valuable than many, has been rebound with a new leather spine and corners.

£300-400

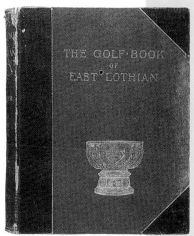

◀ This is the fourth from a limited first edition of 250 signed copies of *The Golf Book of East Lothian* by the Rev. John Kerr, which contained many fine "photographic illustrations" and was published in Edinburgh by T. & A. Constable in 1896.

John Kerr was also the author of *The Golf Song Book*, which was published in 1903 *(see p.68)*.

£1,000-1,500

**FAKES AND COPIES**

There are some counterfeit editions of old golfing books, but with common sense and care, collectors need not worry about fakes. Remember that genuine old books willl have some outward signs of wear and tear – for example, rubbed pages and creased or distressed spines. Be suspicious of apparently old books in pristine condition, unless authenticity can be guaranteed.

▼ Published in 1902, this was the first practical book on golf to be written by a woman for women. It was not, however, the first book on golf written by a woman. That honour went to the poignantly entitled *The Sorrows of a Golfer's Wife* by Mrs Edward Kennard.

£90-125

▲ A great classic that is quite hard to come by, *The Royal and Ancient Game of Golf* by Harold Hilton and Garden Smith, was first published in a limited edition of 900 in 1912. Here too, the head and tail illustrations in each chapter were drawn by Harry Rountree. This copy is number 24.

£300-700

▼ One of the few true classics, and an essential component of every serious collection, Bernard Darwin's *The Golf Courses of the British Isles* was first published in this edition in 1910 with 64 coloured prints by Harry Rountree.

£300-450

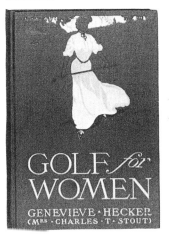

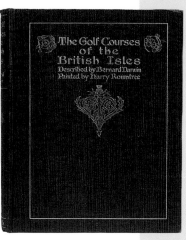

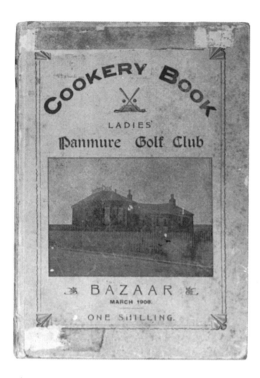

▼ "J.H." Taylor, one of "The Great Triumvirate" with Harry Vardon and James Braid won the British Open five times, but his 1943 autobiography, even in its dust jacket, is not worth as much as Vardon's *(see facing page).*

**£60-85**

GOLF
MY LIFE'S
WORK

J. H. TAYLOR

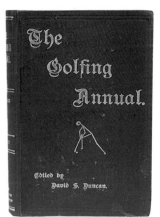

▲ The golfing annual came out every year between 1887 and 1910. A full set could cost up to £6,000, and individual copies, even when like this one, they have been restored, are still comparatively expensive.

**£200-300**

▲ Although few club histories are worth collecting, some club publications are valuable and highly sought after simply for their charm and individuality. This cookery book, by Ms E. Dickie, was specially published for the Panmure Golf Club Bazaar.

**£250-350**

▶ Joseph Murdoch's great bibliography is an essential part of every serious golfing library, and a valuable one too, if it is a 1968 first edition and still has its slipcase, as this one does.

**£200-300**

◄ **Although it has not been signed, this 1933 first edition of a book by the man who won the British Open a record six times, is still a valuable collectors' item, particularly when it has retained its dust wrapper.**

**£120-200**

▼ **This little masterpiece by a friend of Robert Louis Stevenson was published in Edinburgh in 1887. It is one of the best written and most entertaining books on the game and was the first to use photographs to demonstrate technique. It was reprinted in 1983.**

**£300-500**

## CONDITION

Before buying any book for a collection it is important to check the condition. If it is still in its dust jacket, which makes the book more valuable, this must be removed in order to ensure that the cover is clean and not faded, and that the spine is complete and not bumped top and bottom. It is also a good idea to check whether the frontispiece is intact. Usually the most valuable books are signed first editions which still have their dust jacket or slip case, but the collector must make sure that the signature is authentic, perhaps by comparing it with a photocopy of a verified example.

## AREAS OF COLLECTING

Many collectors specialize in particular areas of golfing books, such as biography, fiction, humour, course architecture, handbooks or yearbooks. Others concentrate on some of the most admired and prolific golf authors such as Bernard Darwin, golf correspondent for *The Times* and *Country Life*, or Horace Hutchinson, the amateur champion who also edited the golf volume in *The Badminton Library*, or one of the more recent writers, like the immensely popular broadcaster Henry Longhurst.

▼ **Published as long ago as 1934, this is the rarest kind of first edition. Not only is it autographed, it is also inscribed for the photographer who provided the illustrations.**

**£150-300**

# *Calendars*

By the beginning of the 19th century, long before the era of sponsorship, the image of golf was already so attractive and powerful that it had become a popular theme for calendars among advertisers whose products and services had no real connection with the sport.

Some, inspired by the silversmiths, produced "perpetual" calendar stands in metal, wood or card, in which the same sets of numbers, days and months could be used year after year. Others produced large cards each year with the months printed around the illustration or else attached to the card in a book of "tear-off" slips.

Among the latter, some of the most sought-after are in the series which The Life Association of Scotland produced between 1892 and 1916. The first two in the series, depicting the links at St. Andrews and North Berwick, were painted by J. H. Blair, but the remainder were all by the Edinburgh artist Michael Brown, whose originals, when they can be found, now sell for sums in excess of £20,000. With the exception of two (1908 and 1909) all calendars in this series were illustrated with landscapes of famous courses or of groups of golfing personalities.

Most of the excellent prints from card calendars have been cut out and framed, but those that retain their printed surrounds are valuable and of particular interest to collectors.

◀ The lady golfer captioned "Fore" is one of the famous "Christy Girls" painted by F. Earl Christy between 1890 and 1915. These elegant American subjects can also be found on golf postcards and magazine covers. This one appeared on a calendar and postcard issued in 1902 by S. P. Robie of Lewiston, Maine.

**£30-50**

▶ This delightful calendar, *The Golf Girl*, was given as a gift by the First National Bank of Dwight, Illinois, in 1909. The calendar itself, in the form of a detached, tear-off book, could be replaced each year.

 **£30-50**

◀ Reg Carter, who was well known for his postcard illustrations, also designed this cardboard stand with a small space for a calendar which could be changed each year, hence the 365 on the sand box. It was first produced around 1920.

 **£35-60**

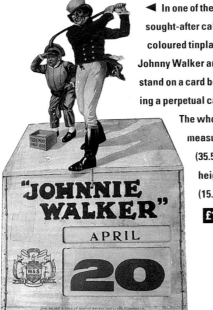

◀ In one of the most sought-after calendars, the coloured tinplate figures of Johnny Walker and his caddy, stand on a card box containing a perpetual calendar. The whole piece measures 14in (35.5cm) in height and 6in (15.2cm) across.

**£150-250**

◀ One of the most decorative examples, this chromo-litho calendar, with the book of months removed, was issued by Eusebe Therrien for 1910. It measures 14 x 8in (35.5 x 20.3cm).

**£300-600**

▼ North Berwick Links, "Perfection Bunker", was The Life Association of Scotland's calendar for 1910. The figures represented are Ben Sayers, R. Maxwell, who was the 1909 Amateur Champion, and the Rt. Hon. A.J. Balfour MP, then

Leader of the House of Commons.

**£200-250**

▼ The Life Association of Scotland calendar for 1913 depicted The Hon. Osmund Scott, The Hon. Denys Scott, Captain Molesworth, Horace Hutchinson and Captain Prideaux Brune approaching the fourth hole at Westward Ho! in Devon. This was the fourth of only six calendars in the famous series that were issued in colour: all the others were sepia.

**£300-550**

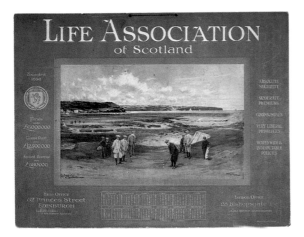

▶ This French calendar on stiff board, 8 x 5in (20.3 x 12.7cm), issued in 1923 by L'Almanch des Postes et des Telegraphies, is yet another example of the huge variety of companies and public services which had taken up the theme of golf.

**£650-850**

# Cigarette Cards

Cigarette cards, which evolved from promotional trade cards and cigarette packet stiffeners, were first issued in Great Britain and the United States towards the end of the 19th century.

The first sets to feature golf were issued around the turn of the century. W. & F. Faulkner led the way with a set of 12 colourful "Golfing Terms" in 1901, followed in 1904 by Cope Bros. & Co. Ltd. who issued a series of 50 "Cope's Golfers". This superb set, originally painted in watercolour by George Pipeshank, is like a *Who's Who?* of early golf in miniature! Great names including Tom Morris, Horace Hutchinson and Andrew Lang, appear alongside such characters as King Charles I wielding a golf club, and other "Golfers of the Old School". Today this much prized set of cards will cost £2,000–2,500.

During the next 40 years, the manufacturers issued a further 37 sets devoted to golf, covering all aspects of the game, from practical to comical. Cartophily has now become so popular that prices have been rising rapidly over the last 10 years. So, to satisfy demand, some older sets have been reproduced, and some new ones have been added, such as for the Panasonic Open (1989) and the Ryder Cup (1991).

▲ Cope's "Golf Strokes" set, containing 32 cards showing leading players demonstrating different strokes, was published in 1923. At 31½ x 18in (8 x 4.6cm) they are larger than the usual 26½ x 14in (6.8 x 3.6cm).

**£175-225**

▼ The most prolific publishers of cigarette cards, Churchmans also produced a set of 25 "Sporting Trophies" in 1931.

**£10-15**

◄ Old Tom Morris, the father of golf, from Churchman's set of 12 "Famous Golfers" first published in 1927. This set proved so popular among Churchman's smokers that a second set of 12 was issued in 1928.

**£175-225 the set**

CHURCHMAN'S CIGARETTES

T. D. ARMOUR

◀ In 1931, three years after the second edition of their "Famous Golfers" series, Churchmans published 50 caricatures of "Prominent Golfers". This popular set was reproduced in 1989. These are usually easy to spot: not designed to deceive, the cards will say that they are reprints or reproductions.

**£225-350**

▼ James Braid, Harry Vardon, Tom Morris and John Ball, photograph cards depicting four great champions from Ogden's Tabs "General Interest Series F", issued in 1903. This series contained 420 different subjects, of which 15 were golfers.

**£175-225**

H. Vardon
OGDEN'S CIGARETTES

J. Morris
OGDEN'S CIGARETTES

James Braid
OGDEN'S CIGARETTES

Mʳ J. Ball
OGDEN'S CIGARETTES

R. T. JONES

▼ Cigarette manufacturers were not the only companies to attract customers with cards. This one is from a series issued by the Goudey chewing gum company in Boston in 1937.

**£15-30**

SPORT KINGS GUM
GENE SARAZEN

◀ As with all other objects connected with Bobby Jones, one of the most popular golfers among collectors, the card depicting him in the 1926 "Who's Who in Sport" series commands a premium.

**£15-25**

**CONDITION**

Cigarette cards must be in near mint condition to be valuable. A "fresh" card with sharp corners and no creases or marks is a far better investment than one in a lesser state. As the first and last cards in each series tend to be those that are most often lost, they usually command a slightly higher price than the others. Cards should be kept in a special acid-free plastic holder, or else mounted and framed. They must never be stuck down, as this damages or even obliterates their printed backs and therefore utterly destroys their value. Fortunately this also means that set of cards glued into their specially-produced printed albums can be obtained for a fraction of the price of a loose set.

# Greeting Cards

The exchange of illustrated greeting cards on special occasions is a very old custom. Even in ancient times the Egyptians and later the Romans gave each other symbolic gifts inscribed with good luck wishes at the start of each new year; and in the 15th century European wood engravers produced inscribed prints for presenting to friends both at Christmas and on New Year's Eve. But it was not until the 1860s that greeting cards began to be made in commercial quantities.

In the 1890s, however, just as the golfing boom was beginning to influence the designs of cards, the British and American industries crumbled in the face of much cheaper imports from Germany, particularly Bavaria. Most of the early greeting cards with golfing designs are therefore German, but the market does not yet seem to have woken up to this and the rare early survivors from Britain and the United States are not noticeably more expensive.

From 1900 until 1914, the Germans had a near monopoly of the greeting card industry, but with the outbreak of the First World War the British and American industries revived and flourished and the growth of their extraordinary market has continued ever since.

For Valentine cards see pp.58–59.

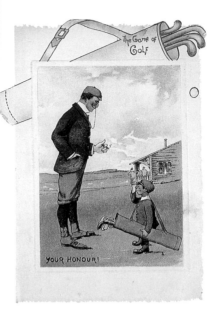

▲ The earliest German cards, such as this one, which was printed in the early 1890s, were single sheets, like postcards, and were designed to be used on any occasion. In this case, a hand-written message on the back shows that it was used at Christmas.

**£12-18**

▼ In the 1920s, confident in its continuing expansion, the British greeting card industry produced large numbers of comic golfing Christmas cards like this one.

**£7-12**

◀ Produced in 1914, this Christmas card already has the nostalgic image and sentimental poem that were to become typical in war time. This example, known as a "song card" because the poem could be sung along to the popular tunes of the time, was produced by Bamforth.

£12-22

◀ By 1918 British manufacturers were making cards once again. This Easter card from 1918 was produced by one of the leading makers, Raphael Tuck & Sons. Between the wars Tuck became one of the largest card producers in Europe.

£8-14

▶ Printed around 1890 in England, this beautifully coloured and embossed card is one of the earliest examples of the influence of golf on the design of greeting cards. "Reward of Merit" cards such as this one, were given to children by their schools at Christmas time.

£20-35

▶ A rare British-made Christmas card from 1913, this one may have been specially ordered as it has the address of the Grand Hotel, Bristol, printed on the inside.

£12-18

◀ Golfing birthday cards are highly collectable. This typical 1920s example was printed by Burn Brothers. The image of the "Golfing Girl" was fashionable throughout the decade, and was popular with illustrators on both sides of the Atlantic.

£8-12

◀ This all-purpose German card from around 1900 has the folded shape that is familiar today, together with a message added by the London outlet of the Bavarian manufacturer Ernest Lister. While an expert chromo-lithographer, it is clear that Lister was not a golfer: this player would need plenty of "Good Luck" with his apalling stance and lazy grip!

£18-25

# Valentine Cards

Valentines are at least as old as any other greeting cards. They were probably first made for the Roman feast of the Lupercalia on 15 February, when young men drew the names of girls from a love urn. The tradition continued into the Middle Ages, when the Christian Church transferred it to the feast of the martyred Saint Valentine, on 14 February, and in the 16th century it was replaced by the custom of giving cards, which has survived to this day.

When golf began to influence the design of greetings cards in general and Christmas cards in particular, it also influenced Valentines, and some of the best early examples are the results of the design competitions which were held first by Louis Prang of Boston, "the father of the Christmas Card", and subsequently by Raphael Tuck in England and Hallmark Cards in the United States. The appeal of golf valentine cards for collectors is easy to see: they are attractive and amusing, and also an affordable item of golfiana.

▲ Doll-like faces were a feature of American Valentines in the 1920s: this one is from 1926. She is a very good caricature of an American golfer of the period.

**£12-18**

▼ A decade after the end of the First World War, Raphael Tuck was again printing cards for the American market. This typical combination of suggestiveness and coyness was made in 1928, and has an innocence not often seen in American cards.

**£10-15**

◄ The couple from Tuck's 1911 card *(see facing page)* appear again in a 1912 card, which was also made in Saxony. This time, however, the embrace is more intimate as the card was made for export to the less formal United States. This card lacks the charm and innocence of the cartoons and other illustrated examples, and consequently is less valuable.

**£8-14**

◄ **Copyrighted in 1911 by John Winsch, this elaborate embossed Valentine card, like most in the United States at the time, was printed in Germany for the American market. A good quality card, it was probably relatively expensive at the time.**

**£12-20**

▼ **During the 1930s the doll-like figures on American cards became much more elaborate. On this card the bag of clubs moves and the right eye winks. Cards like this are a little more expensive than most, but they are still not difficult to find.**

**£18-30**

## GOLF AND ROMANCE

The glamorous image of golf seemed irresistible for the manufacturers of valentine cards in the early part of this century. On both sides of the Atlantic it was presented as a fashionable and youthful game for those with money and style. The leading players of the period, such as Walter Hagen, Bobby Jones and Henry Cotton, were afforded the same status as film stars by many. This image of golf was also adopted by many contemporary advertising campaigns *(see pp. 62–63)*.

Even golfing terms became innuendoes for lovers, as seen in the poems that appear inside many golfing valentines. For example, one rhyme encourages a reluctant male suitor to "putt" the question to his sweetheart!

◄ **This Valentine postcard was issued by the leading British company, Raphael Tuck, in 1911. Nevertheless, like most of its contemporaries, it is in fact German and was specially printed for the company in Saxony.**

**£10-18**

# *Magazines*

The rapid spread in the popularity of golf at the end of the 19th century coincided with advances in the technology of colour printing and in particular with the expanding use of offset lithography. With the availability of cheaper printing and a growing number of affluent readers, magazines became more numerous and their covers more colourful; and as in every other field, golf, with its sophisticated, high-society image, became a popular theme for the decoration of those covers.

To the editors and publishers, the often excellent artwork was simply fodder for an insatiable market. Most of the originals were thrown away soon after publication; and so few records were kept that more often than not the names of the artists have been lost. But the end products have survived in their thousands to create one of the largest and most important fields of interest for collectors of golfing memorabilia.

◀ At the end of the 19th century there were scores of specialist magazines with comparatively small circulations which decorated their covers with golfers, usually young ladies. The May 1899, issue of *The Ledger Monthly* is surprisingly typical.

£45-75

▶ In the 1930s golf and the *New Yorker* magazine shared the same sophisticated market, and the game appeared regularly in the humorous drawings on the magazine's cover.

£38-55

Beginning **The Peddler**—By Henry C. Rowland

◀ Family and weekend magazines such as *Colliers* and *Saturday Evening Post* are another rich source for the collector. This cover is a cut above most, however, as it is painted by Norman Rockwell. By their nature, magazines are not designed to last: to prevent fading, they must be stored carefully, preferably in plastic wallets in dark, dry conditions.

£50-85

◀ Outside the world of purely sporting magazines, golf has always made its most frequent appearances on the pages and covers of country magazines, such as *The Field* and *Country Life*, and general interest magazines such as *Life* and the picture or colour sections of Sunday newspapers. This one sells at a slight premium, however, as the hero in the picture is none other than Bobby Jones, who had come to Chicago to captain the American team in the 1928 Walker Cup.

£120-250

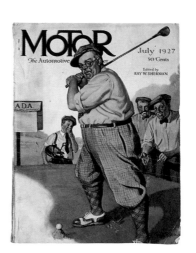

◀ This is an extreme but not unusual example of the influence of a golfing theme. There is not a word in this edition of *Motor* about golf, but the golfing joke on the cover makes it attractive to golfing collectors as well as magazine collectors. It is interesting to note that advertising agents even today continue to use the "image" of golf to sell cars, either to emphasise the higher social status or sporting aspirations of the owner of the vehicle in question.

£45-80

▶ *Judge* was another very popular American magazine which regularly carried golfing covers, and they were usually of a very high standard, like this cartoon by Jefferson Mach III from the edition of 4 August 1928.

£40-68

▼ In highlighting the article "A Comedian Sees the World", the cover of the September, 1933, edition of *Woman's Home Companion* carried a picture of Charlie Chaplin accompanied by a splendid Indian bearer. Among the luggage, the artist included a bag of golf clubs, and in so doing he brought the edition within the scope of the modern golfing collector and made it that little bit more valuable than other contemporary magazines.

£55-90

◀ Golf was a popular theme with European magazines in the 1920s and 30s, but examples of golfing covers on the more "up-market" magazines such as *La Vie Parisienne* are generally rarer and more expensive.

£65-100

# *Advertising*

Manufacturers and their agents have always demonstrated great ingenuity and originality in devising striking advertising for equipment and other golfing products. But the game has also featured in a much wider range of advertising campaigns. Since as early as the 1890s, manufacturers whose products have no connection with the game have nevertheless been eager to associate them with its perceived sophistication and exclusivity. Through changing times the image of golf has always been expensive, and today it is still a regular theme in advertisements for everything from clothes and cars to food and drink.

Some manufacturers even give their products golfing names, and some produce special promotional material in association with particular tournaments. In 1993 Schweppes created tomorrow's collectables when it celebrated the British Open by producing three mini cans decorated with the designs of the courses at St. Andrews, Royal Birkdale and Royal Troon. However, like all promotional cans and bottles, these will lose most of their value if they are ever opened.

▲ The Coca Cola Company has used golf regularly in its advertising. This is an early example from around 1905.

£35-70

▲ Many of the expensive advertising pictures issued by the whisky distillers were extremely stylish. This excellent muted example, 18 x 30in (45.5 x 76cm), first appeared in about 1910.

£300-500

◄ This original plaster of Paris figure, known as the Dunlop Man (16in, 40.5cm), first appeared around 1910. Later and less valuable versions, although just as well painted, are slightly smaller, and the modern versions are so vividly coloured that it is unlikely that anyone would mistake them for the originals.

£300-400

▲ Often known as "The Silver Queen", this is a difficult item to find. Made in fragile papier mâché to promote the Silvertown Company's "Silver King" balls, it was issued in limited numbers between about 1914 and 1920.

£350-500

▼ The landscape of the highland links and the golfing fashions of the early 1920s were an irresistible combination for this Scotch Tweed showcard, which measures 11 x 16in (28 x 40.5cm). This is a high quality example of a piece of golf-based advertising that is relatively inexpensive – the theme has been used a great deal this century by the cloth industry in general, and especially the tweed industry.

**£70-120**

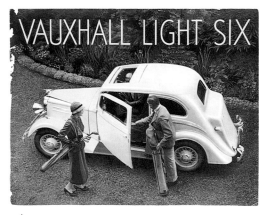

▲ The "Summer" and "Sunday" golf bags and the models dressed expensively in the height of fashion add an air of style and sophistication to the illustration on the cover of the brochure describing the Vauxhall Light Six, which was issued in 1932. Even if they are to be framed, illustrations such as this should never be detached from the rest of the brochure. If they are, they lose most of their value.

**£30-60**

▼ This illustration comes from the inside of a cardboard box that is 5 x 8in (12.5 x 20cm). The box was designed to be left open on the counter of a shop, so that the wrapped biscuits inside could be sold individually. The well-known image of a golfing lady was also used on postcards and blotters.

**£35-55**

▲ This high quality French display card, advertising A. Meiresonne's Golf range of soft drinks, is dated 1934 on the reverse side and was made to hang on the wall of a shop, bar or cafe. After the First World War, enthusiasm for golf spread throughout Europe. France produced some international golfing stars, and the popularity of the game led to its use in advertising.

**£150-225**

# *Postcards*

Postcards were introduced in Austria in 1869. A year later, when the British Post Office followed the example, there was such a demand that the police had to control the crowds. At first the cards were blank and designed to have the address on one side and the message on the other, but by the end of the century picture postcards had been introduced throughout Europe and a craze for collecting them soon followed, and special albums and magazines were published for collectors. By 1909, when the craze had reached its height, the British post office was handling an average of 16 million cards every week.

There are now over 6,500 golfing postcards alone. As a result, most golf collectors specialize in particular topics, such as views of courses and club houses, advertising, photographs and portraits of famous players, comic cards and caricatures. The best places to find cards are the fairs held throughout Britain, particularly the London fairs, which are held in Bloomsbury on the third Sunday of every month, and Bipex, the largest fair of all, which is held in Kénsington every September.

As always, condition is important, but a used card does not have to be in mint condition, so long as it is not creased, torn or dog-eared.

*Golf Club House. Elie.*

▲ Old cards of lesser known golf clubs are as popular with collectors as views of the famous buildings. This one shows the Elie club house in East Fife around 1910.

**£4-6**

▶ The famous firm of Valentines was one of the pioneers of picture postcards in Britain. This one, a classic photograph of Old Tom Morris, was published at the end of the 19th century.

**£18-28**

GOLF NOTES
THE TEE

THERE'S nothing like pluck
If a winner you'd be
So make a good start when you
get to the TEA

◀ The six "romantic" chromo-lithograph cards published by B.B. London at the turn of the century were printed in Germany and were very high quality, which may be why so many have survived. Each postcard showed two lovers accompanied by a piece of doggerel based on a painful golfing pun.

**£10-15**

A tous les âges de la vie, l'HEMOSTYL du Docteur ROUSSEL donne des forces.

▲ Some of the most attractive cards feature 1920s Art Deco drawings, particularly those by French artists, such as Rene Vincent's advertisement for l'Hemostyl du Rossell.

**£8-10**

▼ In another classic photograph of all-time greats, this time from the Wrench series published around 1895, Horace Hutchinson prepares to tee off while Old Tom Morris watches in the foreground on the left.

**£18-25**

Mr. H. G. Hutchinson.
Amateur Champion 1886, 1887.

The Wrench Series, No. 1902

▶ Much less unusual than the French advertising card, but equally attractive to the golfing collector, this advertisement from the 1930s for the Wilson, Weston Sporting Goods Co. of Chicago shows another golfing great, Gene Sarazen, enthralling the eager technical staff.

**£15-25**

GENE SARAZEN AND THE WILSON TECHNICAL STAFF AT WORK IN THE GOLF CLUB FACTORY · WILSON-WESTERN SPORTING GOODS CO. CHICAGO

▼ Many collectors frame complete sets of cards and hang them on their walls. These cards were only produced as recently as the early 1980s, by Morton Olman of Cincinnatti, but they are already much sought after. Excellent, scaled-down reproductions of the eight golfing personalities in the long and famous series of lithographs that first appeared monthly in *Vanity Fair*, they are the work of the greatest Victorian caricaturist, Sir Leslie Ward (1851–1922), who drew under the pen name "Spy".

**£25-50 for an unframed set**

◀ Picture postcards have always been a popular form of advertising with all kinds of companies. This rare, early example (c.1910) was published by the railway company operating between the ports of Liverpool, Heysham and Stranraer.

**£30-50**

# Scorecards & Rule Books

To many collectors, scorecards and rule books are the essence of golf and its history. Even the most simply-used scorecard tells the story of a game and usually something about the club that issued it as well. On the whole, the most valuable are those that were used at the most important tournaments and signed by the most famous players. But, at the other extreme, the most basic unused cards, showing no more than the name of the club together with the outward nine and inward nine holes, are also of interest to collectors. For example, some specialize in collecting cards from all the clubs in a particular area or country; others collect the novelty cards that were given away by advertisers, such as those on the back of some cigarette packets.

Many collectors specialize in the pocket scorers made to be used more than once. These come in a variety of designs and materials, ranging from paper and plastic to precious metals.

Even more than the scorecards, the rule books reflect the history of the game, recording the changes that have been made over the decades, and many collectors attempt to assemble one complete sequence. As with other items, age, condition and the name of the club that issued it, will affect the value of a rule book.

▼ An official scorecard signed by Billy Burke and George von Elna from the 35th U.S.G.A. Open in 1931. The cover shows the local rules, which are of interest because they give a vivid picture of the course, and the completed score side shows a narrow, 76–77 victory for von Elna.

£35-50

◄ The "U.C." Golf Score Card, measuring 2¼ in (5.7cm) square, was made from mother of pearl around 1900. It can be used for stroke play or match play and also has an erasable scoring card on the reverse. This one, still in its box, looks as though it has never been used.

£140-250

▲ Many of the scorecards and score books printed by the tobacco companies have survived. This typical example, from Goodbody's of Dublin, has four pages for scores and eight coloured advertisements by Dudley Hardy.

**£30-50**

▼ Typical of its time, this very plain and flimsy rule book was brought out by the publisher of a catalogue, *The Sports Trader*, in 1912 with the authority of the Royal and Ancient Golf Club. It measures 4 x 8in (10 x 20cm) and its pages have turned slightly brown with age.

**£15-24**

◄ At the beginning of the 20th century, when the Germans had a near monopoly on the postcard market, some of the cards were printed as invitations, with a score card on the reverse side together with a space for the name of the course and the time and date of the match. This unused example in excellent condition was printed in Bavaria in about 1905.

**£20-35**

◄ This 12-page edition of the rules adopted by the U.S.G.A. was published in America in 1918. Like many other booklets and magazines, it could easily be framed, but most of its value will be lost if it is not kept complete.

**£22-35**

▼ The five comic pull-out lessons in *The Compleat Golfer* published around the end of the First World War, included one on the rules. It is now very unusual to find this full set intact.

**£25-40**

► This very popular and highly sought after book of penalties and etiquette with illustrations by "Maxfli" (Harry Rountree) was brought out in 1920 by the Golf Ball Sales Department of the Dunlop Rubber Company. It measures 2½ x 4in (6 x 10cm).

**£50-75**

# Sheet Music Covers

From the last decade of the 19th century until the mid-1930s the sales of sheet music were as important to the music industry as the sales of compact discs are today, and as in so many other fields the sophisticated image of golf was used to sell the product. In all there about 50 musical publications with golfing themes on their covers, even though many of the songs themselves have nothing to do with the game. They range from single songs and tunes without words, most of which were printed in America, to whole books of golfing songs, such as the collector's most valuable musical prize, the *Golf Song Book* published in 1903 by the Rev. John Kerr, who also wrote *The Golf Book of East Lothian*. When it can be found, his song book sells for between £800 and £1,200.

Some enthusiasts collect sheet music for the artwork alone. Others are interested in the music itself, usually specializing in a particular period. To both groups, however, few covers are valuable unless they are complete and in first class condition. Even when the covers are framed, they must never be detached from the remainder of the music.

◀ Most of the music covers in the 1920s were monochrome pen and ink drawings. This one, produced in Newark, New Jersey, in 1928, is unexceptional because it is printed in only one colour, but it is a typical example. **£15-25**

▶ This early example of piano music for *The March of the Golfers* from 1903 is much rarer than its contemporary *The Caddy (see below)* and consequently much more valuable. However, it is a typical example of an early 20th century music cover. **£70-100**

◀ This very early pen and ink cover by Owen T. Reeves Jr. for a comic song *The Caddy*, is strikingly simple and effective. The song was published in New York in 1900, but surprisingly the sheet music is not particularly rare. Finding a copy in good condition is an excellent and relatively inexpensive way of adding an early example to a collection. **£28-40**

ON THE LINKS
WALTZ
FOR THE PIANO
JOHN DUNN.

▶ The *Wannamoisett Waltz*, published in New York in 1915 and dedicated to the Wannamoisett Country Club is typical of the popular illustrations of its period. Although it shows some wear, it is rare enough to be worth buying. Few collectors are going to be lucky enough to find one in better condition.

**£35-70**

THE WANNAMOISETT WALTZ
W.H. PETERS
ELISE GASKILL
HAL FRYER PUBLISHING CO
PROVIDENCE. R.I.

▲ The rarest and most sought-after golf song covers of all are those printed in the 19th century, especially if they were not printed in the United States (as so many were). This extraordinary example is both: it was published in about 1895 in Edinburgh, when the city was already an important centre for golf literature and the manufacture of golf medals and equipment.

**£100-180**

MY LUCKY STAR
FOLLOW THRU
DE SYLVA, BROWN AND HENDERSON SONGS

◀ In 1928 all the songs from the musical *Follow Through* were published on their own in similar covers with the names of the different songs at the top. This one, *My Lucky Star*, is one of the most famous and popular numbers. It is therefore one of the most common survivors and has to be in mint condition to have any value.

**£5-12**

▶ This romantic song, published in 1927, had nothing to do with golf, but to the illustrator the game was part of the image of an ideal American family's lifestyle. Consequently, the cover for this song, written for Babe Adler and her Minstrel Boys, is valuable to the modern collector of golfing memorabilia.

**£12-22**

I'M GONNA SETTLE UP
"THEN I'M GONNA SETTLE DOWN"

▶ The genuinely comic song *I've Gone Goofy Over Miniature Golf* was published in Denmark Street, in the heart of London's music industry in 1930, when the heyday of sheet music was entering its twilight years.

**£5-12**

I've Gone Goofy Over Miniature Golf

# *Stamps*

As they are relatively inexpensive, stamps are an item of golf memorabilia that are within the reach of all collectors. Stamps with golfing themes and images were first issued in the 1950s, and while they do not always have a particular relevance to the sport itself, they are always intesting. Major tournaments often prompted a series of stamps, and at the British and U.S. Open Championships there were usually booths selling specially-printed envelopes for "first day covers", and where these are also signed by one or more of the players, they become extremely valuable, not only to stamp collectors. Unfortunately, however, due to the high costs, the British Post Office was forced to discontinue the issue of stamps and envelopes in 1993.

Golfing stamp collectors have their own International Philatelic Golf Society, which holds auctions and publishes a bi-monthly magazine, *Tee Time*.

A new item for collectors which has emerged from the Open is the commemorative telephone card. The first of these were issued at Muirfield in 1985 and already they are very valuable. An unused and mint £10 card, of which only 750 were issued, is now worth between £800 and £1,000.

CLUB EL RINCON

▲ More valuable than most, this limited edition first day cover was issued by Colombia for the World Cup Golf Championship in 1980.

**£7-12**

▲ In the United States no citizens other than presidents can appear on stamps, until ten years after their deaths. So far there have only been three, and they have all been golfers: Bobby Jones and Babe Zaharias in 1981, and Francis Ouimet in 1988.

**£2-4**

◀ One of the very few triangular golfing stamps, this is another issued solely to earn revenue from collectors, this time by Cook Island.

**£2-4**

▼ Many small countries earn revenue by issuing stamps in celebration of events with which they have no real connection. These stamps were issued by Bhutan in 1984 for Donald Duck's 50th birthday, but were not used until 1991.

▼ In 1978, to celebrate the centenary of the Royal Jersey Golf Club issued a set of four stamps honouring the islands most famous golfer, Harry Vardon. This one was entitled "Grip and Swing": the others were "Golf Course Plan", "Grip and Putt" and "Accomplishments".

▲ In 1975 Jamaica issued a set of sporting stamps which included this golfer. Often when stamps like these come up at auction, the golf collector has to buy the whole set just to get the golfing stamp.

▲ In 1980, in a campaign to promote the resort Sun City, Bophuthatswana issued this stamp of the great South African golfer Gary Player.

▼ This stamp from a sports set issued by Ecuador in 1975, features an unusual picture of an ancient Indian swinging a club.

▼ The island of St. Vincent issued this proof sheet of eight famous golfers for no particular reason in 1992. The full sheet of four stamps is more valuable than if they were collected individually.

## COLLECTING

Golfing stamps can be divided into two categories. Some sets are specially designed to celebrate the game, and feature specific golfing subjects such as those from Jersey featuring Harry Vardon *(see left)*, and other centenary stamps. Others, still of interest to collectors, have a more coincidental connection with the sport. For example, the Republic of Mali issued a series of stamps in 1973 commemorating the Apollo XIV space mission, with one showing an astronaut holding a golf club.

Any collection of stamps should be stored properly. Sticking a stamp down can ruin it, thus reducing both its value and interest, so the best method of display is inside transparent pockets.

### FAMOUS GOLFERS

# Autographs and Letters

The most enjoyable way to acquire the autographs of modern golfers is to collect them in person, ideally by attending the important tournaments and waiting for the stars at the practice grounds. However, collectors can also obtain the signatures by writing to the players or their agents or by swapping with other collectors; autographs of current golfers can be bought from dealers, who also sell the rarer and more expensive autographs of great players from the past.

Autographs are usually more desirable on photographs or programmes, but are most valuable on letters. The value of letters can be increased with the name of the recipient, and even the subject matter. The most highly prized are those that are hand written on headed club or company paper, from one famous golfing personality to another concerning some important sporting event. Autographs of famous golfers in their memoirs can multiply the value of the books, especially if accompanied by an inscription to another famous player.

A good way to start is to buy a history of golf listing all the champions, and concentrate on the winners of one or two competitions, working backwards, so that a collection can be built up quite quickly and inexpensively.

▼ Collections can appear in unexpected places. Here the blank pages of *In Praise of Golf* hold the autographs of 24 players, with each page allotted to a different tournament.

**£145-225**

▼ This portrait of Tom Morris at St. Andrews, dated 1901, is valuable in its own right, particularly as it is signed by the photographer. With a great golfer's signature, it becomes especially sought after by collectors of both photographs and autographs.

**£750-1,150**

▼ This unusual centre spread from a programme of 1952 carries the autographs of Bernard Darwin, the famous golf correspondent of *The Times (see p.51)*, and

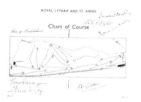

six players, including Gene Sarazen, Henry Cotton, Fred Daly and Henry Bradshaw, who was Irish Native Professional Champion ten times between 1941 and 57 and once played a ball which had landed in a bottle, smashing the glass and moving the ball over 25 yards.

**£300-450**

▲ Full sets of the autographs of members of a team are more valuable on one sheet than they would be if they were collected individually. This collection of autographs of the British Ladies' Team in 1931 is especially valuable, however, because the signatures appear on the menus for the dinners celebrating their departure and return from their U.S. tour, and because this trip laid futher foundations for establishing the Curtis Cup.

**£100-160**

▶ Not all hand written letters are expensive. This reasonably-priced example was written by author and cartoonist, the late George Houghton.

**£60-85**

▼ Like photographs, the usually less costly postcards can be made much more valuable by the addition of an autograph. This example, signed around 1920, shows Alex, or "Sandy", Herd, who won the British Open in 1902 by beating the great Harry Vardon by only one stroke.

**£65-125**

▶ Hand written letters by Bernard Darwin are among the most sought after of those letters not actually written by great golfers. This one, complete with its envelope, was written to the poet Gerald Bullet.

**£75-125**

## AUTHENTICITY

Although forged signatures do not yet present a big problem to collectors of golfiana, it is always sensible to inquire about the provenance of an autograph. The auctioneer or dealer should know where the autograph came from, and whether or not it is likely to be genuine. It is also useful to carry a photograph of an authentic signature for comparison when hunting for a particular autograph. This can help identify forgeries and secretaries' signatures (autographs that have been signed by the players' secretaries on their behalf), which are often stylized and easy to detect. So far, famous golfers have tended not to use automatic signing machines. Fortunately, however, most facsimile signatures are easy to spot, being a flat colour that is totally different to the colour and depth produced by a hand-written, pen and ink example.

# *Blotters*

In the days when everyone wrote with pen and ink, the blotters that were essential on every desk were a particularly inexpensive and effective way for advertisers to keep their names in front of the customers. Like calendars, they were ever-present, but they were likely to be looked at many more times in the course of each day, and they were much cheaper to produce. As with calendars, a wide variety of companies who had no connection with golf used it as a theme on their blotters in order to associate their products and services with the sophisticated image of what was regarded as an elite and glamorous sport.

Golfing blotters seldom bear unique decoration, images were often borrowed from existing products. For example, J.N. Desch's "Golfing Girl" *(see right)* was also found on magazine covers, fashion plates and advertisements.

► This is an unusually luxurious blotter made in 1916 by Thomas Forman & Sons for the British Industries Fair at the Victoria and Albert Museum. It is made in the form of a hardback book with silk bow ties in the spine which hold 16 replaceable sheets of blotting paper. The picture in the oval cut out on the cover is hand-painted on silk.

**£35-55**

◄ Issued in 1940, this is one of the last generation of blotters and it is unusual in that it did not come from a large company. In the darkest moment of the Second World War, in an unfashionable commercial area of bombed-out London, where there can have been very few residents who had ever played golf, a little shop was still handing out optimistic blotters to its customers.

**£9-15**

► Tailoring has often associated itself with the image of golf, and examples are not hard to find, although this one is particularly good. The cartoon is in the style of Lawson Woods and the blotter is one of a set of four issued by Alexander Schneider in 1927.

**£8-15**

## Alexander & Schneider
### Exclusive Tailors
Are a Lot Better Tailors
Than Golfers

Phone 61-111

930 Peach Street, Erie, Pa.

The image of golf has also been consistently popular with rail, travel and holiday companies. This blotter is a little more interesting than most, however: it is dated April 1939, and is among the last of its kind. Already few holidays were being advertised in Europe; the era of the blotter was drawing to a close.

£12-18

▲ Painted around 1918, the "Golfing Girl" was a well known and popular image, which appeared many times in different advertising media during the 1920s.

£9-15

◄ An up-and-coming Hollywood actress and the image of golf were an ideally glamorous combination for a dry cleaner in the 1920s. As part of their marketing campaign for a new movie and a newly featured starlet, Paramount probably let the advertiser use the photograph for no more than a nominal fee.

£7-10

▶ In 1926 the Keystone Emery Mills, who could claim no connection with golf, combined a blotter with a calendar, decorated the card with a portrait of a golfing lady and even added a punch hole so that it could be hung on a wall. However, as with most blotters, the main criteria for determining value are simply the condition and the quality of the artwork.

£7-10

▼ Sutton & Sons, the "Turf experts", who certainly had a connection with golf, produced this expensive blotter at the end of 1922. The cover is made of Bakelite and there are pegs to hold the blotting paper in place. As very few photographs have survived from this period, advertising items like this can also be a valuable pictorial record of the game.

£40-70

# *Ephemera*

In golf as in almost no other sphere of collecting, everything has a value to somebody. To the collector of golfing ephemera, the field is limitless. It can range from objects that others collect, like first day covers, match books and boxes, letters and newspaper cuttings, to score pads for bridge and packages for razor blades or hairnets. No matter how valueless an object may appear, it is worth at least something to the collector if it has even the remotest connection with the game.

The other great joy for the collector of ephemera is that the hobby is not expensive. Some items, like first day covers, can cost no more than face value, and yet in most cases they will be an instant investment. Others will never be worth more than a few pence, but are easily found and inexpensively bought in jumble sales or in attics. Thus ephemera makes an ideal starting point for new collectors on a limited budget.

▶ It is still quite easy to find the Victorian cut-outs of golfers and golfing animals, used for making collages in books and on screens, and most of them, in good condition, can be bought for £8–12. This one in very good condition, advertising Spalding golf balls and clubs, was originally given to professionals and is much rarer. It is 4½ in (11.4cm) high.

£50-80

▲ As with all publications, the value of British comics depends on their age, rarity and condition, and where the cover has a golfing theme, the golf collector will step in to rival the comic collector. This copy of *The Beano* from 8 July 1958, would certainly have an appeal for both fields.

£3-5

▲ First day covers – envelopes carrying new stamps which have been franked on their first day of issue – have always been particularly valuable to stamp collectors. For collectors of golf memorabilia, the value and attraction of a stamp with a golfing theme can be enhanced by a similarly commemorative envelope. This one, carrying the 18 cent stamp issued in 1981 in honour of Bobby Jones, was mailed on the first day of issue from Pinehurst, N. Carolina the home of the Golf Hall of Fame and the new Otto Proust Golf Library.

£7-12

▼ Made in the United States in the 1920s, cards such as this originally carried hair nets, but the design was clearly aimed at men rather than women and intended to persuade them to buy the nets for their wives.

**£12-18**

*What have you there?*
*Some good hair nets my wife asked me to get so that she could play golf without a confounded hat on!*
© M. M. R. Inc.

▲ A perfect illustration of the variety that comes under the heading of ephemera, this elegant drawing formed part of the endpapers in a travel book.

**£5-10**

▲ Elegant enough to be framed as a miniature, this large decorative cigar label is typical of many that were produced around 1910. It is, however, in unusually good condition and consequently quite valuable.

**£18-25**

▼ Illustrated matchbox labels were first produced in the early 19th century. Like the subsequent book-match covers, they are often difficult to date, but this little chromo-litho label, "Don't worry – use a Niblick", is one of the first with a golfing theme and was produced around 1890.

**£10-15**

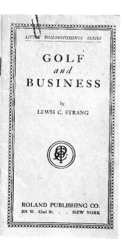

▲ Pamphlets are often among the most fascinating ephemera. This eight page essay on *Golf and Business* was published by Lewis C. Strang in the 1930s.

**£14-22**

## AREAS OF COLLECTING

Generally speaking, collecting golfing ephemera is not perceived to be as glamorous as collecting the paintings and pieces of silver or porcelain that celebrate the sport. However, ephemera is equally relevant and rewarding to collect.

One can learn a great deal about the development of the golf from ephemeral material, and therefore, unless a collection is intended to be specific, it is a good idea to consider collecting everything connected with the game, even down to the smallest items, such as sweet wrappers and cigarette packets with golfing themes.

Modern ephemera should not be overlooked: it is affordable and easy to collect, and may increase in value in years to come. Auction catalogues for golfing sales are a good example, they are already of interest to collectors as they make excellent reference books.

# Silver & Metalwork

In the last quarter of the 19th century golf clubs began to present a huge variety of trophies, medals and prizes made out of precious and semi-precious metals. By the end of the century, most of the objects presented as prizes had also found their way into every high street jewelers shop and silversmiths; and today, the many that have survived, ranging from tableware and ornaments to inkstands, watches, pocket flasks, match safes and all kinds of accessories, make up one of the richest fields for specialist and general collectors on every size of budget.

When examining metal objects, it is useful for the collector to be able to recognise the marks which identify the type of metal and often its date and origin as well. Many reference books exist for this purpose.

As early as 1300, English silver was asayed at the Goldsmiths' Hall in London and stamped with marks which guaranteed its quality. Since then almost all English silver has carried "hall marks". There are usually at least four of these. The first identifies the town or hall where the silver was assayed. the second affirms the quality: for example, a lion represents "sterling" silver, which is 925 parts pure silver to 75 parts of another metal, usually copper. The third is a letter which identifies the year; and the fourth is the set of initials identifying the silversmith. It may be a good idea to carry one of the commonly-available pocket books containing most of the common British hallmarks when visiting auction viewings, markets and dealers. In the rest of Europe and the United States, however, there was never any regular system of marking, which makes identification much more difficult, although many American pieces carry the maker's name and also the word "stirling" which identifies a slightly less pure mixture than the British one. By the time silversmiths had started to make golfing items, the old type of silver plate, Sheffield plate, had been replaced by a new process known as electroplating. As with sterling silver, most British items carry a mark identifying the type of plate: E.P.N.S. for electro-plated nickel silver, E.P.B.M. for electro-plated base metal, and E.P.C. for electro-plated copper.

Other materials employed by craftsmen of golfing metalwares include bronze, spelter and pewter. Bronze was used mostly for statuettes, which were issued in limited editions and signed by their sculptors. These pieces were usually expensive and were often commissioned by golf clubs and associations, as well as enthusiastic individuals, and then used as presentation pieces or for decoration. Spelter and pewter, less expensive metals, were used for less valuable items and often to make mass-produced copies and reproductions of higher quality pieces. For example spelter copies of bronze figures are decorated with a coloured patina to simulate the effect of bronze. Pewter was used in the manufacture of tankards and other tablewares with golfing themes.

---

*(left, top) Silver spoon with a golf ball on the handle, hallmarked Birmingham 1906; £60–90*
*(left, main) Silver statuette of amateur champion F. G. Tait, c.1900; £1,800–3,000*
*(above) Silver spill vase in the shape of a thistle with four clubs and four balls, 1917; £180–300*

# *Sculpture*

The earliest known golfing statue is a bronze of the author and amateur champion Horace Hutchinson which William Tyler made in 1890. In the early decades of this century, however, many small bronzes of leading players or imaginary characters were being commissioned by clubs and commercial enterprises as well as by the players and their families. Some were produced in limited editions and presented as trophies, but many more were used in large quantities on the edges of ashtrays, ink stands and book ends.

Golfing sculpture is one of the few areas of art that is faithful to the technicalities of the sport. This is because, rather than being stylized representations of golfers, the stance, grip and swing of sculptured figures were usually modelled on those belonging to actual golfers, such as Horace Hutchinson, known for his skill at driving and his flamboyant play, and Bobby Jones, famous for his flowing rhythmical swing.

The value of statues and statuettes can vary enormously. Although most of the best are cast in bronze, there are many others made of silver, ivory, copper, brass, tin iron, various other alloys, wood and even papier mâché.

► This German statuette was produced in quite large quantities in the 1930s. Like many others made at the time, it is mounted on a wooden stand and moulded in an inexpensive alloy known as pot metal. Most German statuettes, like this one, were silver plated, but a few exist that were hand painted. The club has been bent, but it could easily be straightened by a silversmith and the flaw has little effect on the value.

**£400-700**

◄ The value of a statuette is influenced as much by the subject as anything else. This is a rare representation of John Ball, the first Englishman to win the Open. He was born in 1861, won his first Amateur title in 1888, won both the Open and the Amateur title in 1890 and played his last Open at the age of 65.

**£800-1,200**

▼ Many figures made in the last 60 years are mounted on marble. This one is moulded in spelter, an alloy of zinc, and it is so well sculpted that it is still valuable despite the replacement club.

**£200-300**

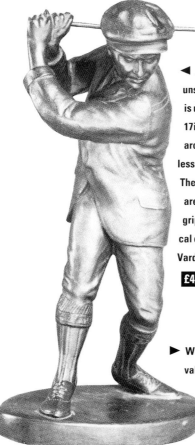

◄ Although it is unsigned and the subject is unknown, this rare 17in (43cm) bronze from around 1905 is nevertheless a valuable work of art. The detail and movement are outstanding, and the grip and stance are typical of the legendary Harry Vardon.

**£4,000-7,000**

► The combination of rarity, a great name and a famous foundry can increase the value of a statuette enormously. This 15in (38cm) bronze of Glenna Collett, six times U.S. Women's Amateur Champion, was struck by the Gorham Foundry around 1926 and modelled by its leading craftsman, E.E. Codman.

**£4,000-6,000**

► Wood does not have the value of precious metal or even bronze, but on the other hand a wooden carving can only be unique. This is a portrait of Captain A.A. Scott, DSO, RN, Secretary of the Royal Ashdown Forest Golf Club. It was carved by Ralph M. Burton in 1970.

**£400-700**

◄ Typical of the 1920s but much more stylish and life-like than most examples, the Art Deco "Golfer" is modelled in ivory and cold-painted bronze and signed by C. Preiss, who was the leading golfing sculptor of the time.

**£2,000-2,600**

## COLLECTING

Some of the best old statuettes are being reproduced in bronze today, using moulds made from the originals. They are even being stamped with their original identification marks. Collectors should buy only from a reputable source and, as always, they should ensure that they have a receipt which includes a full description of the article.

# Silver Spoons & Flatware

Silver spoons come in such a wide variety of shapes and styles, and are so easy to display, that they are among the most popular objects with all silver collectors; and so many have been designed with a golfing theme that there is now a large and growing group of collectors who specialize in these alone.

One of the best and least expensive ways to lay the foundations of a spoon collection is to collect the spoons which many golf clubs still award as monthly prizes. The tradition began at the beginning of the century, and members often compete keenly to collect a complete set of six before a new design is introduced. The names of the winners, the occasions and their scores are often engraved on the reverse of the bowl.

Other silver spoons which can form an inexpensive basis for a collection are the ones which Churchmans cigarettes used to give away between 1933 and 1936 to customers who had smoked a given number of packs. Today, a set of six can be bought for as little as £35. They will cost more, however, if they are still in their presentation box, and even more if accompanied by the original slips of paper congratulating the customers on their "achievement".

▶ "The Golf Girl", a sterling silver spoon, 3½ in (9cm) long, made in the United States around 1900. This example is superior to many other golfing spoons, which are just ordinary shapes with motifs applied to the handles.

**£85-150**

▼ The variety of items which have been made with a golfing theme is almost limitless. Made in about 1930, this sterling silver America lemonade spoon has a long hollow stem which can be used as a straw. This is an example of more unusual golfing flatware. Other pieces include sugar tongs, paper knives and manicure sets. Similar items were featured by Mappin & Webb Ltd, the Royal Silversmiths in their advertisements of Prince's Plate "Golf" wares at the end of the 19th century.

**£50-110**

◀ A typical Birmingham product, this silver cake fork from 1931 was probably originally one of a set. Inexpensive but effectively-engraved items such as this, can often be a good beginning to a collection.

**£30-55**

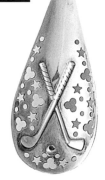

▼ Typical of the type used as a monthly club prize in the first quarter of this century, this standard silver spoon has been given a golfing theme by the addition of an enamelled shield, and is hallmarked London, 1918.

**£60-120**

◀ This very large silver teaspoon, weighing 1½ oz (42.5g) was made by Robert Scott and assayed in Glasgow in 1914. It retains its original leather presentation box, which adds to the value. Spoons similar to this can be found, with bowls embossed or engraved with golfers or clubhouses, but these are quite rare.

**£65-135**

## CONDITION

Worn flatware can suffer a serious drop in value, especially as restoration is almost impossible. On spoons, check the shape of the bowl to make sure it hasn't become distorted through erosion, or thin from being reworked. Forks sometimes have their prongs altered when they become thin or worn. It can be difficult to tell when this has happened, except by comparison with a fork that you are confident has not been altered.

▼ This high-quality silver butter knife with a mother-of-pearl handle in the shape of a golf club is particularly rare: mother-of-pearl was very seldom used on golfing jewelry and silverware. It was hallmarked in Edinburgh in 1927.

**£75-160**

▲ With two crossed clubs and a ball, even a pickle fork can be given a golfing theme. This one is marked Chester, 1922.

**£35-75**

▼ Few silver spoons are more delicately chased than this exquisite pair hallmarked in Birmingham in 1910 and 1912. Each contains 1oz (28.3g) of silver, and is 3¾ in long. They are hallmarked B.M, which suggests that they may have been commissioned and imported from Germany by Berthold Muller, a leading importer.

**£90-150 each**

# Smokers' Paraphernalia

At the end of the 19th century there was a huge boom in the production of decorative but useful objects for the rapidly increasing numbers of gentlemen who smoked pipes, cigars, cheroots and cigarettes, and even for the few "daring" ladies who had begun to smoke. As with so many other similar objects, the makers soon began to add designs and decorations that identified their products with different organizations, regiments, clubs and sports, and golf was a theme that proved to be extremely popular.

In the early part of the 20th century, all the leading companies were making articles for smokers designed and decorated with golfing designs. Indeed, the cigarette companies themselves soon took up the theme of golf to promote their products; an advert for Cavanders' Army Club cigarettes in *The Illustrated London News*, 22 March 1919, is one example.

These items have always been collected, but in recent years with the decline in the habit of smoking, many more have been appearing on the market; in spite of this, prices have tended to increase as there is a growing number of avid specialist collectors. One of the most popular items in this category is vesta cases *(see pp.86–87)*.

◄ This small, white-metal cigarette box, measuring only 3 x 6in (7.5 x 15cm), is dated 1939 and carries exceptionally delicate and detailed relief work. It is extremely unusual to see a case of this quality made in an inexpensive metal. It may have been an apprentice piece or a prototype for a silver model which was never produced because of the Second World War. The decoration chosen by the maker is very traditional. The embossed golfer on the box is more typical of a player in 1910 than one in 1939!

**£100-180**

▼ This elegant silver desk-top match holder and striker was assayed in London in 1922. The attention to detail suggests that the

silversmith who produced it had a good knowledge of golf and equipment. The bramble ball is moulded like an early Haskell ball, and the clubs are technically correct and even have grips.

**£160-275**

▼ This is the sort of well-made object which still offers exceptional value to collectors. Made around 1950, the white metal cigarette box has a wooden lid with a five iron (or mashie) and what could be a Spalding ball with diamond markings.

£25-50

▼ E.P.N.S. Johnny Walker cigarette cases are as sought after by collectors today as they were by smokers when they were first issued. This one, made about 1910, is particularly well preserved. The silver plate looks almost new and, unusually, there are no age marks on the picture.

£150-250

▲ In the 1930s many ordinary pewter ash-trays were embellished with golfing models. This one has a huge, almost life-size mesh ball with four tiny wooden clubs.

£30-50

▼ It is now unusual to find sets such as this in one piece, although a large number of them were made. The ball-shaped lighters have become so popular that they are often missing.

£20-40

# *Vesta Cases*

Among the most common pieces of smokers' paraphernalia made between the 1870s, and the early 1900s were the match safes or vesta cases which were used to contain wooden matches and usually had a rough patch on which these could be struck. Like the lighters which succeeded them, they ranged from expensive, elaborately decorated and personalized pieces of jewelry to cheap trinkets given away by tobacco companies as advertisements.

Vesta cases were usually compact and light-weight, being small enough to slip into a waist-coat pocket. Others were designed to be hung from the chain or "albert" of a gentleman's pocketwatch. Many were silver, though some were made of gold and others of base metals.

Collectors should be careful, however, when buying vesta cases which have been richly engraved or enamelled. This is one of the few areas in the world of golf memorablia where the manufacturers of fakes have been hard at work. Sometimes old cases with genuine hall-marks have been embellished with additional decoration in order to increase their value.

◀ This vesta case is typical of the best cases made in the United States in the 1890s. The beautifully chased golfer may well have been modelled on Horace G. Hutchinson. Only 1¾in (4.5cm) high, the box is made in sterling silver and carries the famous lion, anchor and capital "G" of the Gorham corporation on the inside of the lip.

**£200-350**

▼ Using the most common shape for vesta cases, the British Law Fire Insurance Co. produced an enamelled case in 1902 with a golfer on one side and an advertisement on the other. Although typical of the types of case being used widely for advertising at the beginning of the century, this is better quality than most, as the base and the lid are made of silver.

**£130-240**

▲ Issued in 1900 by grass seed merchants Sutton & Sons, this typical enamelled E.P.N.S. case shows Harry Vardon putting while J.H. Taylor looks on. Although many cases like this were made, only a few have survived.

£180-300

◀ Many vesta cases were made in the shape of balls which opened on a hinge and had a striking area on the base. This one, in sterling silver, was made by Samuel Morden in 1904.

£100-200

▼ Made as early as 1904 for one of the few women smokers, this case has an unusual lid shaped like the top of a heart. It is a little more valuable than most, not only because it is rare but because there is a growing group of collectors who specialize in golfing objects connected with women.

£150-250

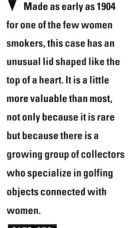

► The most attractive cases are often the simple embossed silver examples with heavy, but uncluttered designs which were made in England during the first dozen years of this century.

£120-225

► This embossed vesta case, made around 1908, is typical of the more elaborate style of decoration that was fashionable in the United States, but at 2¾ x 1½ in (7 x 3.8cm), it is a little larger than average.

£100-200

## CONDITION

Golf-related vesta cases are quite rare and good examples command prices far greater than their "scrap metal value" would initially suggest. Unfortunately, many of the surviving pieces found today are either dented or tarnished in some way, while others, silver examples in particular, have had their decoration and hallmarks literally polished away by well-meaning owners over the years! Collectors of golfiana should be wary of these inferior examples and not be tempted to pay over the odds for them.

# *Trophies*

The first "perpetual" golf trophies, made in the middle of the 18th century, were silver golf clubs to which, each year, a silver golf ball was attached with the winner of the tournament's name engraved on it. By the middle of the following century, however, the most common perpetual trophies were large silver bowls or loving cups. These were engraved each year with the names of their winners and were usually kept at the clubs which organised the annual tournaments. But there are also smaller trophies, often replicas of the larger ones, which the winners were allowed to keep; and in addition, many trophies were awarded to celebrate particular occasions or achievements, such as a hole in one. The best of these are outstanding examples of the silversmith's craft, and many are ingenious combinations of precious metal and equipment, such as golf clubs overlaid with silver and inscribed on the head, or balls mounted in elaborate settings.

Trophies have an added value if their inscriptions associate them with great golfers or other famous personalities, but in many cases it is no longer possible to identify the original winner of a trophy. Where the inscription was written on an added plaque, rather than on the body of the trophy itself, the plaque has more often than not been removed in order to conceal the identity of the vendor.

▲ Like so many trophies, this E.P.N.S. bag of clubs mounted on a plinth has had its plaque removed. Made around 1930, it is much more attractive and better made than most of the similar trophies awarded today and could be used again with a new plaque.

**£80-130**

▼ In many cases the cups awarded as golf trophies were specially made. The emblems of the game were incorporated into the design itself and not just used as engraved decorations on a cup that could otherwise have been used for any sport. This handsome silver example with an air of Art Nouveau was in fact made in 1937 in Birmingham. As it carries no engraved lettering and no longer has its plinth, the competition cannot be identified.

**£180-280**

◄ Another specially-made trophy from 1937, this slim, elegant silver cup is a good example of a design which was very popular in the 1930s and 40s. Cups of this shape appear quite often in the sale rooms, but this one has added value since it was the trophy for the Staffordshire Open Tournament and was won outright with three successive victories in 1949–51 by Charlie Ward, golf correspondent for the *Daily Express* and the *Staffordshire Mail*.

**£150-250**

▼ The rarest and most sought trophies are those awarded at major events. This was the trophy for the *Daily Mail* National Golf Tournament and was made by a leading silversmith, Elkington & Co. The lid is 9-carat gold, hallmarked in Birmingham in 1912, but the body is only gold-coloured metal and the base is silver gilt and wood.

**£5,000-6,000**

◄ Some silver cups made to standard designs were turned into trophies for golfing tournaments by the addition of a figure on the lid. This large (21in; 53.3cm) example is more valuable than most, however, not only because it is unusually elegant but also because it is a rare Masonic trophy, which was first awarded in 1927, with the names of the winning lodges on the plinth.

**£700-900**

▲ Plinths have often been created to carry balls that had been used on special occasions. This particularly elegant example was made in advance to hold the Silver King H.V. ball which Mrs. C. Vernon used in 1937 to "play herself in" as Lady Captain of the Addington Court Golf Club.

**£90-140**

► This 5in (12.7cm) silver tankard, decorated with a bag, clubs and an enamel flag, was made in the United States in about 1900. It is of a type that was often used as a trophy, but, unusually, it has not been inscribed with the name of a tournament, which in this exceptional case adds to its value.

**£400-650**

► Only a few of the replica trophies kept by the winners were as valuable and useful as this silver cigarette box with a relief model of part of a golf course on the lid. Although awarded in 1927, it is hallmarked 1908 and may have been made at the same time as the annual trophy. Replicas are usually smaller than the original, and only bear the details of the winner for one specific year.

**£300-500**

# *Medals*

The awarding of medals to winners of golf competitions is believed to have begun in Scotland during the 1880s and 1890s. Prior to this, trophies took many forms including silver replicas of golf clubs mounted with silver golf balls, championship belts, trophy-cups, rose bowls, and trays. However, few of these were actually presented to the winning players! The introduction of the medal allowed the victorious player to be presented with a token of achievement, while the permanent trophy that had been contested was usually kept on display by the golf club or organization which hosted the competition. Medals soon became the most common prizes for golf competitions in Great Britain, although they were only later adopted in the United States. Most clubs host at least six quality tournaments a year and these, together with the ubiquitous "Monthly medal" competitions, have resulted in the large number and variety of medals available to collectors today.

Most British golf medals were made by the silversmiths of Birmingham, but amongst the rarest are those from Edinburgh where Alex Kirkwood & Son produced some of the earliest examples. Medals were struck in gold, silver gilt, silver or bronze.

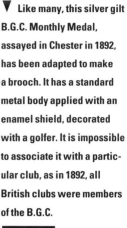

▼ Like many, this silver gilt B.G.C. Monthly Medal, assayed in Chester in 1892, has been adapted to make a brooch. It has a standard metal body applied with an enamel shield, decorated with a golfer. It is impossible to associate it with a particular club, as in 1892, all British clubs were members of the B.G.C.
£150-250

▲ Assayed in Birmingham in 1910 and presented as a "Monthly Medal" in February 1912, this piece, measuring only 1in (2.5cm) across, is typical of the fine silver and enamel work produced in that city at the beginning of this century.
£70-100

◀ This is a silver duplicate – a cliche – of the reverse of the gold medal designed by Benjamin Wyon for the Duke of Buccleuch in 1838. It was made in 1840 for the Royal Perth Golfing Society, still one of the most exclusive clubs in the world, with only 250 members. Cliches such as this were used like any other medals and are equally sought-after. The association with a small, exclusive club adds further to its value.
£150-250

▲ This elegant gold medallion, suspended from a gold cleek and a transitional headed wood made of gold and platinum, was presented by the Neasden Golf Club to Garden G. Smith in 1896, and like most tournament medals, is inscribed with his score – "81 + 2 = 83". Smith was editor of the weekly magazine, *Golf Illustrated*. He wrote a number of books on the game and was contributing editor, along with Harold Hilton, of *The Royal and Ancient Game of Golf* (1912), which is still one of the most magnificent volumes in the whole golfing library.

▼ By the 1920s, golf had become so popular among women players that separate medals were being designed and struck for their tournaments. This silver and enamel example, awarded in 1924, retains its fitted case, which, as always, adds to its value.

**£350-400**

▼ This now rare silver contestant's medal is one of those presented by the United States Golf Association to each amateur who qualified for the national championships in 1894.

**£360-475**

**£350-500**

▼ This 19ct gold Open Championship medal from the Golfing Union of Ireland, enamelled in red, white and blue, has been adapted to make a brooch. Despite this, the value is heightened not only because it retains its original box but also because, uniquely, it is dated 1937 and inscribed to Reginald Arthur Whitcombe, who in fact won the championship in 1936. The competition was played at the Royal Dublin Club, and Whitcombe won the title with a total score of 281, which was then the lowest winning score for any major championship. The author of *Golf's No Mystery*, and *Psychology for Golf*, Whitcombe was the youngest of three golfing brothers. He also won the Irish Open in 1935 and 1939, the British Open in 1938, and was a member of the 1935 Ryder Cup team.

**£800-1,200**

▲ This 15ct gold brooch was presented as a monthly medal to ladies, by Royal Lytham & St. Anne's Club in the early 1920s. The motif of crossed golf clubs was a popular one for golfing medals.

Other methods of decoration included players in midswing, golf club crests and inscriptions. A collection of golfing medals can be a good way of reliving some great moments of the game.

**£160-240**

# Metal Ornaments & Tableware

By the beginning of the 20th century, when many clubs had begun to present silver ornaments or pieces of tableware as prizes in their tournaments, the leading silversmiths started to offer similar items for sale to the growing number of golf enthusiasts.

In the United States, the two most prolific specialists in this field were the Gorham Corporation and Unger Brothers.

The Gorham Corporation was founded in Providence, Rhode Island, in 1813 by Jabez Gorham and four partners. In the 1860s it began to make objects in sterling silver and it continued until 1967, when it was taken over by Textron.

Founded by five brothers, the Ungers began as cutlers in 1872, but soon diversified to include dressing table sets, match-holders, jewelry and other decorative objects. Their most sought-after wares have unusual forms with female figural designs.

▲ This picture frame, 5¾ in (14.5cm) wide and 5¼ in (13cm) high, is typical of the elaborate silver and enamel wares which the Gorham Corporation was producing in the U.S.A. at the beginning of this century. It carries the usual Gorham trademarks – a lion, an anchor and a decorative capital "G".

£600-900

◀ Pieces such as this 1930s silver candlestick holder often have an inflated value, since they are sought after not only by collectors of golfing silver but also by the collectors who specialize in items associated with particular golfing personalities. Here, the figure in the centre represents Glenna Collett, who was U.S. ladies champion a record six times between 1922 and 1935.

£200-350

◀ Most of the Birmingham silversmiths produced ranges of tableware on a golfing theme. This ball-shaped mustard pot, made in 1922, is a good but typical example. It retains its blue glass lining, which protects the silver from the corrosive effect of the mustard, and its spoon, like its handles, takes the form of an iron-headed club.

**£140-240**

▼ This sterling silver blotter, 2½ x 4in (6.5 x 10cm) is much more typical of the Unger factory's products at the beginning of the century. Emma Dickinson, the wife of Eugene Unger, one of the founders, designed a number

of articles in this Art Nouveau style, which became a speciality of the firm.

**£400-750**

▲ This silver and leather notebook and stamp holder complete with its original pencil, made in Birmingham and dated 1905, carries the maker's initials L.S.S. The well-etched golfer in plus fours and a flat cap is not unlike Harry Vardon. Unusually for a silver piece, it carries a registration number.

**£130-220**

▶ This very attractive E.P.N.S. inkstand is typical of the many that were made in the United States at the beginning of this century. The gutty balls on either side of the figure are the ink wells; and the pen is shaped like a club.

**£200-400**

▼ Another object associated with a famous golfing personality, this time British, this silver-topped pin cushion from around 1900, with an alligator leather back measures only 1½ in (4cm) in diameter. The figure in the Art Nouveau frame is Lady Margaret Scott, who was British Ladies' Champion 1893–1895, and famous for a swing so supple that at the top of her backswing her shaft came round her shoulder in a direct line to the ball.

**£50-140**

◀ The delicacy of detail and sense of movement make this statuette an outstanding example of its style and period. It was hallmarked in 1908 and sculpted by Hal Ludlow, one of the leading Art Nouveau silversmiths.

**£1,500-2,000**

# *Jewelry*

Like most golfing collectables, golfing jewelry has been popular since the 1890s. When women played in hats or wore scarves round their necks, hat pins and brooches were essential to keep them in place, and they were made to suit every pocket in everything from gold and diamonds to brass, silver plate and enamel. In the 1920s and 1930s, when jewelry was no longer essential on the links, many more decorative pieces were introduced, and these were often awarded as prizes.

Prior to the Great War, golfing jewelry was also popular amongst gentlemen. Gold and enamel cufflinks, and sets of waistcoat buttons depicting golfers were produced, while others were engraved with the names and crests of golf clubs and societies. Similarly, silver and gold tie pins in the form of golf clubs were fashionable with both golfers and non-golfers alike.

As with so many items of golfing memorabilia, golfing jewelry is sought after by many enthusiasts apart from golf collectors. Many pieces are prized for their craftsmanship by antique jewelry collectors, and many are similarly attractive to collectors of Art Nouveau and Art Deco.

◄ Typical of the hundreds of thousands of pins that were made in the 1920s, this American brass brooch is styled after the Pinehurst caddie boy.

**£40-70**

► An extremely unusual silver pin from the 1920s, this was probably a prototype that was never marketed. The shoulders are hinged on the bow tie, so that the arms can swing across the body to putt.

**£100-160**

◄ A 1980s copy of a 1910 lapel pin or scarf holder. 2in (5cm) long and 1½in (3.8cm) high, it is moulded in metal and coated in silver.

**£15-25**

► On this brooch the charming and humorous rear view of a young caddie has been inlaid in silver on tortoiseshell. After 1910, when this was made, tortoiseshell began to go out of fashion.

**£85-125**

▼ Golfing hatpins, mostly made of silver, were often shaped like clubs, with precious or semi-precious stones as the heads. As most golfing ladies had more than one pin, there were also silver pin holders with golfing designs. As hat pins are still plentiful, and because silver crushes easily, pins must be in good condition to have any value.

**£25-75 plain silver pin**

**£110-160 if before 1918**

### WOMEN AND GOLF

The manufacture of golfing jewelry for women has followed their interest and participation in golf. Golf was played by some gentlewomen in the late 19th century, but the first real boost for female players came in 1893 with the founding of the Ladies' Golf Union, and the first women's amateur championships held at Portrush. From then on the manufacturers of golfing jewelry began to enjoy a much wider market.

◄ This very unusual combination of a bulldog clip and a club brooch looks as though it was made to hold a scorecard. It was hallmarked in Birmingham in 1896 and is signed with the designer's initials.

**£120-180**

► The Art Deco style was particularly well suited to silver jewelry. This charming silver and enamel pin was hallmarked in Chester in 1939 and bears the maker's initials.

**£100-160**

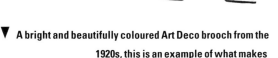

▼ A bright and beautifully coloured Art Deco brooch from the 1920s, this is an example of what makes jewelry so attractive to so many different collectors. The oval image inside the silver frame is made of mother of pearl which has been hand painted and then fired.

**£125-175**

# Clocks & Watches

For the last 200 years, in every sport, club, company and society, clocks and watches have been the most popular gifts for retiring captains and dignitaries, and they have also been among the most popular prizes for champions and other achievers. From the moment the golfing boom began therefore, at the end of the last century, watch and clock makers on both sides of the Atlantic were working eagerly to meet the demand from a constantly growing number of clubs.

The symbols of the game fitted easily with the heavy, over-elaborate, Baroque style that was popular with clockmakers at the time. Soon every important jeweler's shop contained several large metal mantel clocks, often ball-shaped, standing on "grassy" plinths with ball supports, surrounded by collections of clubs and heather, and frequently surmounted by a statue of a golfer. The watch makers on the other hand were more restrained, simply engraving or embossing cases, enamelling faces and adapting their pieces to take on the shape and surface of a ball.

Today the surviving handiwork of these craftsmen, even the most over-elaborate, is particularly valuable, being sought after by collectors of watches and clocks as well as golfing collectors.

▼ Dunlop also gave its name to a range of silvered metal pocket watches for gentlemen.

**£300-400**

▲ Less elaborate than most, this electro-plated clock, made around 1890, was one of the first made in a style that remained popular in the most expensive jewelers until almost 1920.

In the last ten years clocks such as this have increased in value by 600 per cent.

**£1,200-1,800**

◄ Again not particularly elaborate, but nevertheless a disturbing mixture of styles, this valuable brass clock mounted on an ebonized Rococo stand was made at the beginning of the 20th century. The brass clubs and ball combine so uneasily with the ebony Rococo scrolls that it almost looks as though they were added later.

**£800-1,000**

## COLLECTING

Collected mainly for their decorative appeal, most golfing time pieces are fitted with simple standard movements and dials made in Great Britain, France or the United States. Clockmakers were therefore able to concentrate on the quality of the ornamentation, and pieces are sometimes signed by the designer. Those wanting to invest in golf watches or clocks are best advised to buy an example that is in good working order: restoration and repair can be expensive, especially if new parts have to be made.

► In the 1920s all the competitors in ladies' tournaments were sometimes presented with gold wrist watches in the shape of a Dunlop ball with their names engraved on the inside of the protective lid. This one still has its original leather strap.

**£300-400**

► The standard statuette of a golfer, originally moulded for a series of clocks, was often added to other instruments as well. Here he swings a little precariously and incongruously on top of an Art Nouveau metal barometer, which was made around 1910.

**£150-295**

▼ Apart from inkwells, one of the most popular silver items to adopt the ball shape was the watch case, which was used to hold a watch on a desk or bedside table. This one with golf club brackets was made in England around 1910.

**£300-400**

97

# Glass & Ceramics

By the beginning of the 20th century, golf had begun to develop into the well-organized and social game that we recognize today. As the game grew in popularity, so golf became a common theme for different areas of the decorative arts. Pieces found their way into golfers' homes, and ceramics and glassware were also awarded as tournament prizes as alternatives to medals, spoons and trophies.

By far the largest number of golfing pieces were ceramics; the reputation of the game is clearly shown by the number of items with a golfing theme that were made by the major manufacturers of pottery and porcelain. Almost all major British and American manufacturers produced golfing pieces: Series wares and Burslem "Morrisian" wares by Doulton & Co,

Wedgwood's Sports Series and Hemlockware, and the Ceramic Art Company's silver-mounted mugs and jugs. Items have also been produced in places as diverse as Holland and Japan.

At their most basic, golfing ceramics include plates, cups, saucers and other tableware. More unusual items exist such as tiles, biscuit barrels and even bottle-sized spirit flasks. There is a huge range of relatively inexpensive pieces available, and this is an exciting area in which to begin a collection.

At the beginning of this century, when manufacturers on both sides of the Atlantic were producing an enormous variety of golfing ceramics, golfing glassware was by contrast surprisingly scarce. During the 1920s, however, the glass manufacturers of England and the United States at last became aware of the opportunities presented by this still growing and apparently insatiable market. Most of their products were painted, engraved or silver-overlaid decanters and sets of glasses, many of which were used as prizes, but some companies also made cut-glass tableware and occasionally simple ornaments and statuettes.

Players of golf, both real and imaginary have been immortalized in print, moulding and paint on all sorts of ornamental wares. They will often give a sense of the history of the game, showing gentlemen dressed in flat caps and plus-fours, caddies carrying bags of hickory-shafted clubs, and women in long skirts and wide-brimmed hats. In contrast, some pieces commemorate actual events, such as Wedgwood's plate commemorating Neil Armstrong's lunar golf swing!

Golfing glass and ceramics are affordable, attractive and often useful items, relatively easy to find, and fun to collect either in their own right, or as part of a wider golfing collection.

*(left, top) A Wedgwood Hemlockware jug, c.1900; £400–700*
*(left, main) Glass ashtray engraved with a golfer; £40–80*
*(above) Foley/Shelley small cream jug, c.1930; £140–200*

# *Glass*

The large majority of golfing glass has always been relatively expensive, and it is probable that most good quality pieces were either specially commissioned as competition prizes or made exclusively for those with a lot of money. Many items are relatively inexpensive, but prices will increase when the decoration becomes more elaborate, and rare coloured pieces, manufactured in Britain, Europe and the United States, command a premium when they appear on the market.

In addition to cost and rarity, collectors of golfing glassware are hampered by the nature of the glass itself. Unlike pottery and porcelain, broken glass is difficult to repair invisibly and thus is often disposed of when damaged – golfing motifs notwithstanding! It can be stuck or riveted, but methods such as these will leave the glass looking unsightly. Collectors will also need to be wary of some examples which have been cleverly reshaped by grinding, and alterations hidden by mounts or frames.

▲ **This good baluster glass jug made in the late 1930s is decorated in the style of the children's book illustrator Chloe Preston, who also painted a few golfing watercolours.**
**£40-70**

▼ **Frosted glass tumblers decorated with silhouettes were very popular at the beginning of the century. Sometime the silhouettes were portraits or cartoons of real characters specially commissioned by clubs or individual golfers. Comparatively few have survived, however, and this one, made around 1905, is a particularly fine example.**

**£35-50**

◀ **While some 1920s glass manufacturers were making pieces like the blue vase *(see right)*, many others were producing much more elaborate pieces with delicate minutely detailed silver overlay. Decanters like this one, with a long stopper edged in silver and different designs on each side, are still not too difficult to find, and it is often possible to collect matching sets of glasses in different shapes and sizes.**
**£250-400**

◀ This pinch bottle with silver overlay would be desirable enough as an early example if it were only in clear glass, but the amber glass makes it rare and very valuable, not only to golf collectors but also to glass enthusiasts.

**£300-400**

◀ Although painting and engraving were more common, sterling silver overlays were used quite often on the highest quality glass. This 12oz (340g) drinking glass, which also has a silver rim, was made in the United States around 1920.

**£45-80**

▶ An example of the very best in 1920s design, the heavy, dark cobalt blue vase has a subtle, tapering shape and a confidently bold but simple silver overlay running right round it.

**£200-400**

▼ A rare piece of tableware from as early as 1910, this American glass biscuit barrel has been cut in the shape of a mesh patterned golf ball. The fluted tray, the club supports, the ball-topped lid and the flag-shaped handle are all made of sterling silver.

**£400-600**

◀ Made in the 1950s this traditional wine glass has been hand painted in oil and then glazed over. It was originally part of a set of six, each of which had a different golfer on it.

**£15-25**

# Tableware

During the 1890s, when the popularity of golf spread rapidly among the rich, a large number of firms on both sides of the Atlantic produced ceramic wares decorated with golfing themes. As the 1890s were also one of the greatest eras of the society hostess and lavish home entertainment, it was inevitable that many of these firms should concentrate on dinner and tea services and other tablewares, usually made in fine hard-paste porcelain. Many clubs gave single items as monthly prizes, and keen players strove throughout several seasons to collect a full service, just as collectors today assemble the same services piecemeal from markets and auctions. However, surprisingly, the manufacturers seem to have over-catered for the market. By the end of the first decade of the 20th century most of them had withdrawn, leaving the English company Doulton & Co. with a near-monopoly, particularly in tableware. Doulton's most popular golfing products were "Series Wares", in which the same mass-produced pieces were decorated with transfer prints of different golfing themes, including the adventures of Charles Dana Gibson's famous "Gibson Girl" and cartoons by Charles Crombie.

▼ This exquisite and wittily decorated cream jug was made at the Crown Porcelain Company's Burslem works by Susie Cooper, one of the great women potters of the 20th century. Susie Cooper worked for Crown during the late 30s and early 40s, when output was limited by wartime austerity. As a result, examples of her golfing tableware are now extremely rare.

**£100-125 each piece**

▼ Teapots are particularly valuable and sought after, as many porcelain and pottery enthusiasts collect nothing else. This fine example was made in the late 1890s, at the height of a crowded market, by MacIntyre, one of the few firms other than Doulton & Co. to continue production well into the 20th century. The exceptionally animated and well painted golfer was one of the company's most popular and easily recognizable motifs and was used on a wide variety of tableware.

**£175-300**

▲ Some of the finest golfing porcelain was made in Europe for the American market. Sold under the trade name "Schwartzburg", these rare pieces from a coffee service were made in Rudolstradt, Germany, around 1910 by the New York and Rudolstradt Pottery and were decorated in the style of the American artist Harrison Fisher.

£185-750

▼ One of the most popular ranges in Royal Doulton's series ware was based on the illustrations in *The Rules of Golf*, which Charles Crombie produced for Perrier in 1905. The series of tableware, which was made continuously from 1909 until the mid-1930s, included both dinner and tea services.

£300-350

▲ This comparatively rare and valuable Carlton Ware hot water jug, produced by the Wiltshaw and Robinson factory in Stoke on Trent at the turn of the century is usually easy to recognize, as most of it is decorated with the same two golfers and a caddy in the background. Many pieces are marked "Carlton Ware" in script.

£200-300

◄ This delightful small coffee cup and saucer is another example of the quality that makes MacIntyre pieces so popular with collectors. Founded in Burslem in Staffordshire in 1860, the company was taken over by Moorcroft at the beginning of the 20th century, and produced golfing tableware until 1928.

£125-225

► It is fairly easy to distinguish between modern and older Royal Doulton: the mark changed in the late 1950s from a circle and a lion, to a slightly smaller lion. Bunnykins tableware from the 1930s such as this jug, was made for children not golf collectors, so early examples are often worn.

£125-225

# Decorative Plates, Plaques & Tiles

Ornamental plates and plaques are among the most popular items with all collectors of ceramics. As a result, collectors of golfing memorabilia are often in competition with other specialists; and the prices of golfing plates are further inflated by the fact that there are many more enthusiastic collectors in golf than there are in most other sports. This disparity in prices is particularly noticeable in the series of sporting plates which most of the leading factories produced at the beginning of this century: the golfing plates are now almost always more expensive than the plates depicting other sports.

When the late 19th century manufacturers first decorated ornamental plates with golfing themes, they almost always chose the most elaborate designs, such as those with moulded rococo rims; and in the same way the makers of plaques continued the opulent, heavily coloured traditions of the Renaissance majolica makers. Tiles, however, which date back to the 17th century, are among the oldest pieces of golfing memorabilia, and even most of the 20th century examples have retained the simplicity and restraint of the beautiful early Dutch designs.

◀ A perfect example of the simple design typical of Dutch tiles at the end of the 17th century. Tiles like this are now being reproduced and in some cases chipped, aged and sold as originals.

**£300-350**

▼ This large Dutch Delft tile, measuring 6 x 8¾in (15 x 22cm), was made in the mid-18th century. The golfing scene is much more detailed than those on most smaller tiles, but it is also more delicately painted than the average plaque.

**£1,500-2,000**

▼ Here the long-established Neo-classical style for which Wedgwood is most famous has been used to celebrate one of the great achievements of modern science. Actually made in 1972, the plate marks the moment in 1969 when astronaut Neil Armstrong played a golf shot on the moon.

**£150-225**

◄ At the beginning of this century many manufacturers produced sets of six differently decorated dinner plates. One of the most popular was made by Winton Ware for Grimwades at Stoke-on-Trent. The plates were sold in two qualities, heavy duty plates, which were intended for use, and lighter, more expensive versions, such as this one, *Golf Critics*, which had decorated borders and were intended for display.

**£135-250**

▼ In 1931 Wedgwood & Sons produced a very high quality "Sports Series" in which only about two dozen editions of each plate were

made. Designed by Arthur Dale Holland and Kennard Wedgwood, each plate was lightly printed in outline and then hand painted by Dale Holland himself. Few of these plates have survived. Wedgwood made other high quality sport and golfing plates in the 1930s, including the "Etruria Series", but these were issued in much greater quantities and are worth half as much as the "Sports Series".

**£350-550**

► Typically heavy in its colouring, this blue and white Doulton Burslem plaque, 14in (35.5cm) in diameter, was hand painted by one of the factory's leading artists, J. Littler, some time between 1891 and 1902.

**£2,500-3,500**

▼ Made in 1933 to a much older traditional pattern, this is the valuable golf plate from a sporting series of Masons Staffordshire "sampler plates". They were known as "sampler plates" because the illustration in the centre was designed to look like an embroidered sampler.

**£200-350**

► The design of this attractive 20th century tile is very close in concept and restraint to the 17th century Dutch patterns.

**£75-150**

# *Ornamental Wares*

During the 1890s the companies that made tableware began to produce ornamental ceramics, not only in porcelain, but also in stoneware and earthenware; in addition there were companies which specialized in ornamental wares.

In the United States the market leader was the Ceramic Art Company (now Lenox), founded at Trenton, New Jersey in 1889 by Walter Scott Lenox and Jonathan Coxon, while in Britain the most popular wares were produced by Doulton & Co. and Copeland Spode *(see facing page)*. Doulton & Co. (1815–present) dominated the market with a huge range of items, often with golfing motifs. Products include Lambeth Stoneware, "Morrisian" ware, Kingsware and Ornamental Series Ware.

Very few of the early golfing ceramics have been reproduced, and it is usually safe to rely on the standard manufacturers' marks; where these do not appear, styles tend to be easily recognizable.

▶ **A rare piece of Royal Doulton series ware, made around 1935, this is one of four small ashtrays, 1½ x 2½ in (3.8 x 6.3cm), which fit into a ceramic cigarette box. The cartoon transfer is marked with the facsimile signature of the famous H.M. Bateman, whose work was used only on ornamental series wares.**

**£80-130**

◀ **The most extravagant of the Royal Doulton products were the "Morrisian" wares, which were made in limited numbers at the Burslem factory between 1900 and 1924. Highlighted in gold, their shapes and borders followed the designs of William Morris, after whom they were named, and they were decorated with golfers in fanciful 17th century costumes, in the manner of the American artist Will Bradley. Not all the pieces are marked "Morrisian", but the style and quality are unmistakable.**

**£400-650**

▼ The standard of painting on some pieces from the 1890s is as fine as on any English porcelain of the period. This small, rare and elegant biscuit barrel by Wood & Wood was made around 1893 and is decorated with a stencilled and hand-painted scene. The barrel itself, together with its E.P.N.S. lid, stands only 5in (12.7cm) high, and with the handle raised it is just over 7in (18cm). On larger barrels, the handles were often shaped like two crossed clubs.

**£1,000-1,300**

◀ In the early part of this century, many of the small ceramic pieces sold for a few pennies as mementos from holiday resorts were moulded into golfing shapes, particularly balls. Survivors are much sought after by collectors and often command surprisingly high prices. This one was made around 1910 by the Arcadian China Company and carries the arms of Church Stratton in Shropshire.

**£45-80**

▶ The Copeland Spode factory in Stoke on Trent made mostly containers, such as jardinières, teapots, jugs, mugs, ornate decanters and biscuit barrels like this one. The decorations were applied in white relief over blue or green glaze.

**£500-750**

▼ Another company which began to produce golfing ceramics at the height of the market and continued longer than most was the Japanese Noritake factory in Nagoya. This tobacco jar was made there around 1927, and like all Japanese products imported into the United States after 1894, it is marked "Nippon".

**£300-550**

## SPODE (1776–present)

The Spode factory at Stoke-on-Trent in Staffordshire was founded by Josiah Spode. By 1800 it had developed what was probably the first formula for English bone china. In 1813 the founder's son went into partnership with W.T. Copeland, and in 1833 he was bought out by Copeland and T. Garret. The factory has now merged with Worcester, a company which dates back to 1751.

Before 1830 the most common mark was a hand-painted "SPODE", alhtough printed marks did exist by 1820. After 1833 "COPELAND & GARRETT" was written in a circle with "LATE SPODE" in the middle.

# Steins & Loving Mugs

In the last quarter of the 19th century beer mugs, or steins, became the most popular mementos of university fraternities, colleges and clubs. Every university town had at least one shop selling a variety of steins and other tankards, all decorated with the arms of the university or its colleges, and then divided into groups by the emblems of the various sporting clubs and cameos of the different games being played.

The vogue for these steins began, not surprisingly, in Germany, and it spread to Britain and the United States, and this happened at around the same time as the sudden boom in the popularity of golf. While some British and American manufacturers added spa towns and seaside resorts to the list of universities, others added golf to the list of games. One of the first to do so, and soon one of the leaders in the field, was the Ceramic Art Company, later to become the Lenox China Company, although it did not officially adopt the name until 1906.

◄ The Dickensware made by the Weller Pottery in Zanesville, Ohio, at the end of the last century consisted almost entirely of ornamental vases and jugs. Simple beer mugs such as this one are extremely rare.

The decoration was applied by a method known as *sgraffito*. The outlines were scratched onto the soft clay before firing, and afterwards the earth coloured background was sprayed onto the whole surface and the scratched shapes were then filled in with solid colours.

**£500-775**

▼ In the decade following 1899, when Walter Scott Lenox-established the Ceramic Art Company, the Trenton factory produced a large number of high- quality, hand-painted lamps, jugs, mugs and tooth pick holders. They were painted in green or occasionally blue, and many of the steins, like this one, were expensively rimmed in sterling silver.

All Lenox mugs are signed by the individual artists who decorated them and some carry the marks of the fashionable retailers who ordered them in bulk, such as Tiffany.

**£800-1,200**

◀ The O'Hara Dial Company, which made watch faces, also bought steins with plain pewter lids from Lenox and then added a variety of decorations to the pewter. This example bears a portrait of a Native American on its lid. Many of the early golf clubs in the United States were formed by like-minded drinking companions, which explains why the "nineteenth hole" (the clubhouse bar) has always been an important part of golf.

**£800-1,200**

▶ Lenox and several other companies included a few three-handled steins and loving mugs in their range. This blue Copeland Spode loving mug is slightly broader than most, with a diameter and height of roughly 5½ in (14cm).

**£600-1,000**

◀ The more elaborate decorations on Doulton & Co. "Morrisian" wares often had more in common with Aubrey Beardsley than William Morris or Will Bradley. This rare three-handled mug or tyg, remains valuable despite a small repaired chip. A collector will buy such a piece until he has the funds to "trade up" to a perfect example.

**£2,000-3,500**

## DOULTON & CO.

The social aspect of golf has meant that attention has often fallen upon the all-important "nineteenth hole". Manufacturers of tankards, steins and loving mugs were not slow to appreciate this, especially in the beer-producing countries of Great Britain, Germany and the United States.

As with vases *(see pp.110–111)* Doulton & Co.'s Royal Doulton wares offer the most variety to collectors. In particular the stoneware tankards and loving mugs designed by John Broad which were popular between 1880 and 1914. These were decorated with colourful glazes and applied motifs of golfers of the period. Many are silver-mounted, and intended largely as sporting trophies. More recently, Royal Doulton issued a character ale jug, designed by David Biggs, of the golfer of 1971. It is believed to represent W.J. Carey who was chairman of Doulton & Co. in the United States at the time, and presumably a keen golfer.

# Vases

During the last quarter of the 19th century and the first two decades of the 20th, European and American porcelain and pottery manufacturers produced vases in greater varieties and larger quantities than they had ever done before or have done since. Mass produced and decorated with transfers, or hand thrown and hand painted, they were made not only in the contemporary fashions, such as Art Nouveau and "Arts and Crafts", but also in respectful pastiches of all the great styles of the past – Classical, Medieval, Renaissance, Rococo, "Vernacular", and Neo-classical and endless interpretations of Oriental designs and decorations.

When the manufacturers began to extend their range to exploit the growing enthusiasm for golf among their most wealthy customers, they also adapted their vases and decorated them with golfing themes. It was not always a successful marriage. Stout gentlemen in plus-fours looked absurdly out of place amid the curves and twirls of Art Nouveau. But women golfers in long flowing skirts usually seemed much more at home, and the popular pictures of golfers in 17th century costume blended well with the simplest of the traditional Vernacular shapes, and also, surprisingly, with some of the contemporary ones.

▲ At the turn of the century, a number of glass manufacturers produced beautiful hand painted vases, although very few were decorated with golfing images. This fine campana shaped example, which is only 7½ in (18.3cm) tall, has been painted with a copy of one of the most famous of all golfing images, the Blackheath Golfer.
**£250-350**

◄ ▼ These Royal Doulton tablewares decorated with transfer printed illustrations from Charles Crombie's *Rules of Golf*, which were produced between 1909 and the mid-1930s, were accompanied by a wide range of ornamental wares. Here, the comic 17th century figures do not look at all out of place on the tall, elegant vase (left).

**£150-250**

▲ This valuable pair of Royal Doulton "Morrisian"-ware baluster vases *(see p.109)*, each measuring 9in (15cm), feature exotic golfers, and are decorated with gold designs, over a red body and a black neck, that are characteristic of this particular series.

**£800-1,200**

▼ This little (6in, 15cm) pot was actually designed to be a vinegar container and was made in the 1920s as part of a large dinner service by Crown Ducal, which was the trade name of the Staffordshire firm A.G. Richardson & Co. However, most of these pretty pots were used as vases for single flowers and for collectors looking to obtain a complete dinner service, they are among the most difficult pieces to find.

**£100-175**

◄ Charles Crombie's delightful 17th century figures did not fit so comfortably on classical two-handled vases. Nevertheless several patterns were produced, all to a very high standard. Some even had gilt handles. This one, made in 1915, is 11¼ in (28.5cm) tall and has had a black glass stand added at a later date.

**£3,000-4,000**

► At the beginning of this century Royal Doulton made 10in (25.4cm) porcelain vases with silver rims shaped like golf bags. They also made miniature versions which were only 2½ in (6.3cm) high.

**£700-1,000**

# *Figures*

Amongst the earliest ceramic golfing figures are a pair representing William Innes and his caddy, produced at the potteries in Staffordshire in 1905. These figures were drawn directly from Lemuel Francis Abbott's famous 18th century painting of "The Blackheath Golfer". One figure depicts Innes wearing the famous red captain's coat of the Blackheath club, while the other shows his caddy carrying various clubs under his arm – golf bags had yet to be invented!

It is worth noting that despite the game's long history in its native British Isles, most golf figures available to collectors were manufactured by foreign companies. Many of the cheaper mass-produced examples came from Germany during the early part of the century, and from Japan in the 1930s.

An English piece of note is the Carlton china figure of a golfer created by the cartoonist John Hassall, dating from the early 1920s, which has a face in the form of a golf ball! This figure later became a popular car mascot.

**◄ ▲ Popular with golfing collectors, these portly golfers and goofy caddies were made by the Amphora factory in Austria. They come in two sizes, 11 and 13¼in (27 and 34cm). Another famous Austrian manufacturer is Goldscheider who produced female Art Deco golfing figures. These are firm (if expensive) favourites with collectors.**
**£400-600**

**◄ This practical figure from the 1930s, was made in France and is a full bottle-sized spirit flask. The head attaches to the neck with a cork stopper, and the bent arm can be used as the handle. Several European factories made novelty flasks like this in the 1930s.**
**£220-300**

▼ Sold for a few pennies at the beginning of the century as a souvenir of St. Andrews, this white bust of "Old Tom" Morris is now a much sought after collectors' item. It was made by Willow Art China of Longton, stands 6in (15cm) high and has a transfer print of the arms of the city of St Andrews on the front.

**£180-300**

▼ Since the beginning of this century there have been several different Staffordshire groups representing "The Blackheath Golfer" and his caddy. This one, a little less primitive than many, was made around 1930.

**£500-700**

### SHELLEY (1872–1966)

This factory, originally known as Wileman & Co. and later trading under the name "Foley", changed its name to Shelley in 1925 although the Shelley stamp had been used as early as 1910. Known principally for tableware designed by famous artists such as Eva Crofts and Mabel Lucie Atwell, Shelley also produced a number of ceramic figures which have become extremely collectable.

All genuine Shelley wares are marked, most commonly with a script signature inside a cartouche. Anything that is marked "Fine Bone China" will be post-1945.

Shelley designs are characterized by their conventional form and commercial appeal. In contrast, other English manufacturers, such as Burleigh are well known for their innovative ceramic figures.

▲ Modelled on the illustrations of the famous children's artist, Mabel Lucie Attwell, this Shelley Bone China figure *(see text box)*, "the Golfer", is very popular and consequently quite expensive, despite the fact that it is not particularly rare.

**£300-500**

▶ Many of the wares that were made in the 1920s and 1930s, with figures incorporated in their designs were much more lively and imaginative than the ordinary figures. This charming Burleigh Ware jug from the 1930s with the figure of a golfer as a handle, is an excellent example.

**£180-220**

"What should I take here, Caddie?"
"I should take a Guinness, Sir!"

# *Art*

In the 17th and 18th centuries, a few Dutch, Scots and English artists painted golfing scenes and portraits in oils for aristocratic clients. Golfing art did not become available to a wider and less wealthy public, however, until 22 November 1790, when Valentine Green published a limited edition black-and-white mezzotint of the portrait of William Innes, the Captain of the Society of Golfers at Blackheath, which Lemuel Francis Abbott had painted a few years earlier. Not more than a dozen examples are known to have survived, but just over a hundred years later, during the great boom in the popularity of golf, two more black-and-white editions were published in 1893 and 1901. The first coloured mezzotint, by Will Henderson, was published during the First World War, and a second, by Walter A. Cox, was published in 1926. Since then there have been scores of coloured reproductions of one or other of these earlier editions. Although the portrait itself was destroyed in the middle of the 19th century, the image, now known as "the Blackheath Golfer", has become the most famous in all golfing art.

As in every other golfing sphere, the end of the 19th century saw a proliferation of all kinds of golfing art. Portraits, groups and landscapes in oil and watercolours became popular among the rich, and a huge variety of prints became available. Many of the most famous prints were commissioned and published in magazines, and these illustrations are now the most popular and least expensive examples of golfing art. Among the most sought after are the golfing girls of F. Earl Christy (1873–1952), Charles Dana Gibson (1867–1944) and Harrison Fisher (1875–1934), the *Vanity Fair* caricatures of "Spy" (Sir Leslie Ward, 1851–1922), scenes and portraits by Thomas Hodge (1827–1907), cartoons and landscapes by Harry Rountree (1880–1950) and cartoons by Henry Mayo Bateman. Several other famous and highly sought after sets of prints were issued only in portfolios, but some of the most famous, such as "The Seven Ages of Golf" by John

Hassall (1868–1948) and "The Rules of Golf" by Charles Crombie (1885–1967), have often been reproduced, and when the reproductions are sold in frames, they look very like original prints.

Golfing photographs also became popular in the 1890s, but there are many highly sought after examples which were taken earlier. The first professional photographer to specialize in golf, Thomas Rodger, set up in St. Andrews in 1849 and continued to work there until 1883. As with prints, many of the most accessible photographs were used as illustrations, although in this case the best were in books rather than magazines. Among the most admired examples are those in Horace Hutchinson's *British Golf Links*, which was published in 1897.

In the 20th century the field of golfing art broadened considerably. Many of the leading artists were commissioned to paint posters for tournaments, transport companies and travel agents. Apart from original paintings, these are on the whole the best examples of golfing art and make ideal decorations for club bars and studies, and the finest of them are regularly reproduced.

In hardly more than a hundred years, golf has become a sport that is genuinely rich in art.

*(left, top) A comic print by H.M. Bateman for Guiness; £40–80*
*(left, main) A Spanish magazine cover; £55–90*
*(above) The Blackheath Golfer, an engraving by Will Henderson after Lemuel Francis Abbott; £60–100*

# Portraits, Caricatures & Figures

The earliest known golfing pictures are the scenes and portraits that were painted in Holland in the 17th century. It was not until the end of the following century that the first famous portraits were painted in England and Scotland, and during the next hundred years there was very little increase in the demand for golfing subjects. Most of the pictures that have survived from this period are very large portraits of club captains or groups of players. They were commissioned to be hung in club houses or country mansions, and for the most part they are still in their original homes. During the 1890s, however, the demand increased dramatically. Captains, distinguished amateurs, important professionals and members of keen golfing families, including the children, were represented in pencil, watercolours and oils by almost all the leading portrait painters. The famous caricaturists depicted all the personalities of the golfing world, and prints of their work were published in fashionable magazines.

The popularity of golfing portraits has continued ever since – every leading professional can expect to have one painted – and a surprising number now find their way into the sale rooms.

◄ One of the pioneers of the renaissance in golfing art at the end of the last century was Thomas Hodge (1827–1907), a member of the Royal and Ancient Club at St. Andrews, who excelled at both figures and landscapes. His portrait of Old Tom Morris about to play off on the famous course has captured the great man's presence and personality perfectly – but then Hodge and Morris were contemporaries, and may even have played a round or two together! A schoolmaster and an excellent golfer, Hodge also provided illustrations for several publications, including *The Badminton Library*.

**£2,500-4,000**

▼ A good and typical example of the 18th century-style paintings that were so popular at the end of the 19th century, this oil on panel, *The Nineteenth Hole*, has been cut down to fit its heavy frame. It is unsigned, but is probably by a painter in the circle of Frank Moss Bennett.

**£700-900**

◀ This charcoal and body colour caricature, *The Golfer* was drawn around 1920 by Harry Rountree, who was famous both for his cartoons and other illustrations which often appeared in *Punch* and other magazines, and for his landscapes of golf courses *(see pp.118–119)*. Rowntree's work commands a premium, so buying an amusing drawing such as this, is probably the least expensive way of acquiring one of his pieces.

**£800-1,600**

▼ The original drawings for cartoons can be found surprisingly often at auctions. This one, captioned "He only goes round with his wife now", was drawn in ink over pencil around 1890 by Harry Furniss (1854–1925), a prolific and versatile illustrator and cartoonist, who worked for both *Punch* and *The Badminton Library*.

**£300-450**

◀ It is not difficult to find one of the hundreds of amateur or semi-professional watercolour portraits painted in the early part of the century. This one is particularly good and more valuable than most, even though the subject, *The Laird*, and the painter, "R.C." are unknown.

**£400-650**

▲ *Playing for the Pot*, in ink and watercolour, was signed and dated in 1920 by H.M. Bateman (1887–1970). The cartoon was part of the artist's own collection and was not sold until 20 years after his death. Although quite often available, originals by cartoonists as famous as Bateman are always expensive, but are also an investment.

**£3,000-5,000**

▲ Usually, important modern portraits of famous players only come onto the market with the sale of entire estates or collections. This oil of Bobby Locke in his South African blazer, painted by John Berrie in 1949, shortly after Locke had won the British Open, was part of the player's own collection.

**£3,000-4,000**

# Landscapes

The golf boom of the 1890s brought as much new work to landscape artists as it did to portrait painters. Captains commissioned pictures of their courses, and many players wanted pictures of their favourite fairways and greens. Knowing that then as now views of famous courses were as popular as portraits of famous players, several landscape artists travelled round Britain, pausing at each course to paint a few scenes and sell them to the club members before moving on. One of the earliest and finest sets of scenes was the series of 64 watercolours which New Zealander Harry Rountree painted for *The Golf Courses of the British Isles*, which Bernard Darwin published in 1910. To the delight of a few lucky collectors, these beautiful originals do occasionally appear on the market.

Today golfers are still commissioning pictures of their favourite views, and a number of important modern painters are attracted by the ordered landscapes of golf courses. Among those whose work is particularly popular with golfing collectors are Julian Barrow, Graham Baxter, Linda Hartough, Bill Waugh and Arthur Weaver.

▲ **Thomas Hodge's muted and distinctive landscapes are even more admired by collectors than his portraits and figures. This fine view of the Royal and Ancient Club House at St. Andrew's, complete with his affectionate criticisms of the building, was painted in 1879. Hodges, who regularly played golf here, and who won the spring meeting competition in 1861, would have been very familiar with this scene showing the Swilcan Bridge in the foreground. Many of Hodge's watercolours still hang in his old club house. It has only been in the last 15 years that a few from private collections have come onto the market, and they are always hotly contested at auction.**

**£3,500-5,500**

▼ **Painted in 1917 by James Christie Bruce, an artist not noted for golfing scenes, this sombre oil on canvas of the view of St. Andrews from the links, measuring 15.5 x 25.5in (39 x 65cm), is a good example of the very high quality, but relatively inexpensive oil paintings that can still be found on the market.**

**£800-1,300**

▼ A collector's treasure: a watercolour of *Felixstowe Golf Club* by Harry Rountree for Bernard Darwin's book, *Golf Courses of the British Isles*. A prolific author and a successful player, Darwin won a CBE for services to literature and sport in 1937.

**£3,500-5,000**

► Few watercolours can aspire to the sort of prices that collectors are prepared to pay for the works of Harry Rountree. This excellent view of Cooden Beach Golf Club by Sidney Pike is much more within the reach of the average picture collector.

**£500-800**

▼ The golfing caricatures and scenes of cartoonist and illustrator Frank Reynolds (1876–1953) have recently been reproduced in a book. A pair of scenes rather than a landscape, this drawing from around 1930 shows the traditional charm of the

small professional shop, and a prophetic vision of the sale of mass-produced golfing equipment. Reynolds was on the staff of *The Illustrated London News* and *The Sketch*, and was art editor of *Punch* from 1922 to 1932.

**£200-350**

▼ In evaluating a picture and identifying a bargain, a knowledge of golf and its history is as important as an eye for painting. A rare artist or an unusual subject can often add considerably to a picture's value. Nevertheless, it is unlikely that any collector would find anything as unusual and valuable as this on a market stall.

Exquisitely painted in watercolours by Garden Grant Smith in 1892, *Crossing Jordan* depicts the course at the spa town of Pau in southern France. It is one of only a few known paintings of golf in 19th century Europe and it is probably the only one that is ever likely to come onto the market.

Founded in 1856 by the Duke of Hamilton and others, Pau Golf Club is the fourth oldest outside Scotland – after Royal Blackheath (1603), Old Manchester (1812) and Royal Calcutta (1829).

**£15,000-20,000**

# Photographs & Stereoscope Cards

The earliest known golfing photographer was Thomas Rodger, who worked at St. Andrews between 1849 and 1883. In those days it was not possible to print photographs in books: the only way of reproducing them with a printing press was as engravings. As a result, examples of work by Rodgers and his younger contemporaries are now extremely rare and valuable, particularly if they are of famous golfers or groups at important tournaments. Collectors should be wary, however: several of these old photographs have been convincingly reproduced, sometimes using the original glass negatives.

Other photographs which are particularly prized by collectors are the pairs which were made to be used in three dimensional stereoscopes. From the beginning of the century to the 1930s, long before the introduction of instructional videos, many leading players produced complete sets of these to help keen amateurs improve their game.

A collection of golfing photographs is a wonderful way to record the history, fashions and technical development of the game, as well as the famous faces and great sporting moments.

▼ A great moment in the history of golf: after tying in the final of the 1896 Open with Harry Vardon, J.H. Taylor prepares to tee off at the first for the 36 hole play-off.

Needing four to win at the last hole, Vardon had played short of a dangerous bunker and settled for a safe five, before going on to win the play-off by four strokes.

**£125-175**

OPEN GOLF CHAMPIONSHIP MUIRFIELD 1896

▼ Another old group, valuable simply as a charming oddity, this gathering of players, caddies and officials was photographed at an octogenarian foursome match at Royal Musselburgh in 1906.

**£120-200**

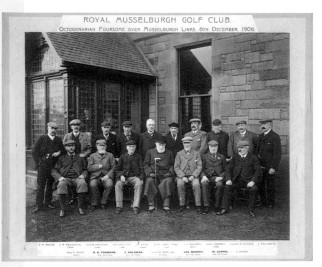

ROYAL MUSSELBURGH GOLF CLUB.
OCTOGENARIAN FOURSOME OVER MUSSELBURGH LINKS, 6TH DECEMBER 1906.

Two stereoscopic cards from sets demonstrating the styles of the stars. Bobby Jones ▲ addresses the ball for a mashie pitch, and a stymied Harry Vardon ▼ pitches his ball over his opponent's. As always, the picture of Bobby Jones commands a slightly higher price.

**£45-75 Jones**

**£40-70 Vardon**

▲ This photograph of old Tom Morris is quite well known and has been used on a postcard. It is of particular interest, however as its value has been almost quadrupled because it is signed. Morris won the Open Championship four times, and was one of the most famous golfers in Britain in the last two decades of the 19th century.

**£1,100-1,650**

▼ Another of the all-time greats, Harry Vardon, in full swing at the height of his career. The photograph was published in London by the Swan Electric Engraving Company in 1905 and it has been signed by both Vardon and the photographer, George W. Beldam. The value is slightly reduced, however, by a scratch and a few creases at the bottom.

**£400-600**

▼ Group photographs, which are an essential basis to any collection, can vary in price from very little to a considerable sum, depending on their date, their location and the number of famous names they contain. This one is more interesting than important. It was taken on the steps of the Royal and Ancient Golf Club at St. Andrews in 1895, and includes Fred Herd who was to win the U.S. Open three years later.

**£250-350**

# *Posters*

The expansion of the railways and the spread of tourism at the beginning of the 20th century were accompanied by continuous and often intense advertising campaigns promoting resorts throughout Britain and Europe and encouraging the public to travel with one of the many rival shipping and railway companies. The main elements in these campaigns were always striking, colourful posters, often painted by the leading artists of the day, and inevitably golf was one of their strongest and most constant themes.

Printed on paper and then mounted on canvas or linen for strength, the posters were made in limited numbers and were mostly pasted onto hoardings. As a result very few of the earliest have survived; and some, particularly those that were issued by now extinct railway companies before the First World War, are much sought after today and can command prices of up to £3,000. However, as in most cases where prices are high, collectors have to be cautious. There are now good modern copies on the market; once framed they are difficult to distinguish from an original, so always check carefully.

▲ **The same size as the Great Eastern poster** *(see below)*, **and promoting the same part of the world, this one was issued only a few years later by the rival London North Eastern Railway.**
**£1,000-1,600**

▼ **Although few examples of each have survived, the French resorts commissioned large numbers of posters from leading artists in the 1920s and 30s. This one was painted by Roger Broders.**

**At an average size of just over 3 x 2ft (90 x 70cm), the French posters are usually slightly smaller than the British ones.**
**£1,000-1,400**

◄ **An example of the most sought after type, although not from the most valuable early period, this large Great Eastern poster, measuring 5 x 3ft (1.5 x 0.9m), is in the style of John Hassall and was issued in the early 1920s to promote travel to the east coast of Scotland.**
**£1,200-2,000**

◄ Walt Disney often included a golfing Donald Duck when drawing personal cartoons and writing autographs, and the combination of Donald and golf, such as on this poster, will always attract collectors.

**£200-300**

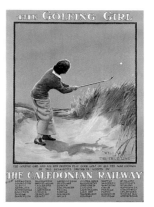

◄ This rare *Golfing Girl* poster was issued by the Caledonian Railway around 1910. This is one of the posters that has been copied, although the modern reproductions are not as large as the 5 x 3ft (1.5 x 0.9m) original.

**£1,200-1,800**

► Some modern posters are also well worth collecting. This one is already rising in value. Not only is it one of a limited edition, it has also been signed by its distinguished artist, Byron Huff.

**£70-170**

▼ Even the world of posters has its oddities. This very rare framed half poster in the style of T. Miya Mago, was issued in Japan in 1954.

**£300-350**

▼ Golf has even found its way into political posters. This rarity, measuring 3 x 2ft (90 x 70cm), was issued in 1910 by the Budget League, which published a weekly magazine

for young men. The objective was to rally support for the prime minister, Lloyd George, whose budget had just been vetoed by the House of Lords.

**£450-650**

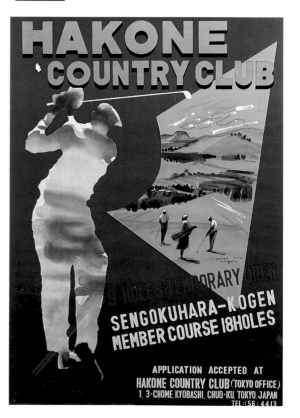

# Fine Art Prints

The first few golfing prints, published between 1790 and 1812, were all mezzotints, engravings or etchings. These were made by marking the images on metal plates, covering them with ink and then pressing the paper onto them. These techniques produce varying effects which can be distinguished using a magnifying glass: mezzotints appear grainy, and engravings and etchings are made up of many small lines.

At the end of the 19th century, when the rapid growth in golf's popularity was accompanied by an increased demand for prints, many of the new generation were lithographs. Originally the image was drawn on limestone using a greasy crayon, in was placed on the dampened stone which only stuck to the greasy areas. Again this required great patience and craftsmanship, and prints were only issued in limited quantities, and they were often numbered.

By contrast, the most common modern method, offset lithography, can produce infinite numbers very rapidly. The printing plate is arranged next to a rubber roller, and it is this that transfers the inked image from plate to paper. The quality of the prints produced in this way is very high, but they are produced in much greater numbers and are therefore less valuable.

▲ Cecil Aldin (1870–1935), who is famous for his animals and light-hearted hunting scenes, also painted a set of six views of golf courses, which were issued as prints. The first, limited editions of only 42 copies of each scene were all signed by the artist and are now greatly prized, not only by golfing collectors. This example shows the Fourth Green at Sunningdale. The others are of St. Andrews, North Berwick, Walton Heath, Westward Ho! and Royal St. George's.

**£400-700**

► Art Deco golfing prints are becoming increasingly popular with collectors, particularly those of Gladys Emma Peto (1890–1986), one of the leading exponents of the genre. Ms Peto was a watercolourist and illustrator and worked for *The Sketch* from 1915–1926.

**£75-135**

▼ One of the most popular and stylish golfing artists at the turn of the century was John Hassall (1868–1948), who published a set of four bright and charming chromolithographs around 1909 entitled *A Drive*, *A Bad Lie*, *Bunkered* and this one, *Putting*.

**£750-1,000 each**

▲ Golfing prints by the 20th century's other great painter of hunting scenes, Lionel Edwards (1878–1966), are as prized by all print collectors as those of Cecil Aldin. This one, *A Threesome*, is a very early example, painted at a time when his style was still very close to Aldin's. Nearly all Edwards' golf subjects have titles with double meanings, and often feature glamorous women golfers in romantic situations.

**£150-350**

▶ "The Christy Girl", painted at the turn of the century by American F. Earl Christy (1873–1952), has appeared in many different poses in prints, postcards and posters. Although not rare, she is highly sought after, particularly by collectors who specialize in prints of female golfers.

**£100-175**

▼ The English landscape artist Arthur Weaver has made a speciality of golf courses, and prints of his work, which are often issued in limited editions, are highly sought after by collectors. As on this print of the 1969 Masters at Augusta, Georgia, they are usually signed and decorated in pencil with a small vignette, known as a remarque, at the bottom.

**£300-400**

◀ Many good prints were issued as advertisements. This mezzotint of a painting by H. Southam, for Canadian Club Whisky by Coupil & Co. was copyrighted in 1898.

**£700-1,000**

# Comic & Satirical Prints

Many of the most popular golfing prints at the turn of the century were comic scenes by famous artists and illustrators such as Tom Brown, H. M. Bateman and Charles Crombie. During the 1970s, when large numbers of golfing prints were reproduced in excellent, inexpensive offset-lithograph editions, the comic scenes were again among the most popular. At the same time, however, a few unscrupulous dealers made high-quality copies of these prints on heavy paper and sold them as rare first editions. When these are in old frames and protected by glass, they are usually extremely convincing, as it is very difficult to judge the age of the paper. Collectors who are prepared to pay the high prices which early prints can now command should buy only from reputable dealers and should always ensure that they have a receipt which gives an exact description of their purchase.

As with all prints, a comic scene is more valuable if it is a numbered print in a limited edition of less than, say, 400, or if it has been signed by the artist, or if it has been embellished with a small drawing or watercolour, a remarque, on the margin or the mount.

► Coy rather than comic, this shows John Hassall in a more sentimental vein. It is one of a set of eight signed prints entitled *The Seven Ages of Golf*, which was published in a limited edition of only 200. For the second edition, only the first print was signed, and subsequent editions were completely unsigned. Apart from this one *The Infant*, the other titles are *The Schoolboy*, *The Lover*, *The Soldier*, *The Justice*, *The Lean Pantaloon*, *The Caddy* and *Early Lessons*.

**£200-300 single print**

**£2,000-3,000 a set**

RULE XX
···· A player
shall not play
until the ···
ball is at rest
under penalty
of one stroke.

"*The harp he loved never spoke again.*"
*The Bootest Boy*

◄ In 1905 the Perrier mineral water company in France published a book of 24 lithographs, *The Rules of Golf*, by the *Punch* illustrator Charles Crombie (1885–1967). The book was such a success that a second edition was published soon afterwards, and the prints have remained among the most popular of all golfing prints. Several offset-lithograph editions have been produced more recently, but these are easy to distinguish from the earlier versions. In the first place their English captions have French subtitles; and secondly they do not have Perrier advertisements on their reverse sides. The first two editions can also be distinguished easily by the position of the copyright notice. On a first edition print, it is at the bottom of the box containing the caption. On a second edition print, like this one, it is below the margin.

**£60-100 single print**

**£700-1,000 book**

▲ *Addressing the Ball* by Victor Venner, which was published as a pair with *Lost Ball* by Richard Wyman in 1903. Venner also painted scenes for the designs on Warwick porcelain plates.

**£300-500**

► In the first 30 years of the 20th century, golf was the excuse for a surprisingly large number of images of women in various stages of undress. This print of two mermaids by Renc F. Outcault, published around 1910, is one of the better known, as it was also used on Belleek porcelain.

**£50-95**

► Louis Wain (1860–1939) was famous for his pictures of cats taking part in different human pastimes. His set of four golfing scenes, which were published in chromolithographs, consisted of *The Drive*, *The Approach*, *The Putt* and *Holed Out*, which is shown here in its rare original golfing frame. Reproductions of these scenes have recently been published, and they sell for one tenth of the price of the originals.

**£200-300**

◄ During the 1890s Cope's Tobaccos commissioned a series of political prints by artist John Wallace, wllo drew cartoons as "George Pipeshank". This one, published in July 1893, while the Irish Home Rule Bill was at the committee stage, shows Prime Minister W.E. Gladstone in a bunker with Irish politicians with his cabinet looking on. Most of the figures can be identified. The caddy (top left) is Joseph Chamberlain; Lord Randolph Churchill is sitting on the edge of the bunker above the prime minister. These prints often appear in the sale rooms, but collectors beware: the whole series has recently been reproduced.

**£400-600**

OLDEST GOLF HOUSE IN AMERICA

# The Great Championships

The great championships are the high points in the golfing calendar, their history is central and plays a major role in the development of the game itself. Many of the keenest collectors make them the focus of their collections, reaching out into all the other fields of specialization, collecting everything from equipment to trophies and from art to ephemera, and assembling and displaying the disparate objects with a tournament, or tournaments as a unifying theme.

The story of the great championships is also the story of the great champions. The first famous professional, Allan Robertson, died in 1859, a year before the Prestwick club offered a belt as a prize for an "Open" tournament, but his even more famous apprentice, "Old Tom" Morris, came second in the first Open, won the second and then went on to win the belt three more times. In 1868, at the age of only 17, Tom's son, "Young Tom", won the first of three successive Opens; and he remains the youngest player ever to have won.

To the collector, the memorabilia from competitions becomes more valuable if it comes from those that saw the setting of new records or other great moments in the careers of the giants of the game. A scorecard, for example, will be much more sought after if it comes from the fourth Open to be won by either of the Morrises, or from the fifth to be won by James Braid, John H. Taylor, Peter Thomson or Tom Watson, or from the record sixth to be won by the great Harry Vardon.

Items from the great amateur tournaments are equally sought after. Indeed the most valuable of all are those connected with the achievements of the greatest of all modern amateurs, Bobby Jones. The smallest

piece of ephemera from the British Amateur Championship of 1930 is particularly valuable, not just because that was a year in which it was won by Jones but because that was the unique year in which Jones also won the British Open, the U.S. Amateur Championship and the U.S. Open.

The Opens, the Masters, the Amateur Championships and great team events like the Ryder Cup are obviously the most popular specializations, but there are many enthusiasts who collect items from the other tournaments on the U.S, European and other P.G.A. Tours.

To many collectors, the significance of most championships is that they are regular events and collecting related memorabilia is an on-going process, year by year or championship by championship. These days most championships have associated "villages" close to the courses where all kinds of merchandise, souvenirs and promotional material can be obtained.

*(left, top) Oil painting of Ian Woosnam winning the Masters at Augusta, 1991, by Paul Gribble; £800–1200*
*(left, main) Poster commemorating the 90th anniversary of the U.S. Open in 1986, signed by Byron Huff; £100–140*
*(above) Winner's gold medal from the US Open, 1898; £10,000–20,000*

# Open Championship Memorabilia

The British Open Championship is one of the great golf tournaments. Many collectors specialize in the wide variety of objects which commemorate them, and the most sought after are those associated with the tournaments that have been milestones in the history of the game.

The first Open Championship in Britain was held between eight professionals in 1860 over three rounds of the 12-hole Prestwick links in Scotland. The winner, who held the Championship Belt for the first year, was Willie Park Sr. of Musselburgh. Although many amateurs entered in the following year, the winner was another professional, Tom Morris Sr, and between 1868 and 1870 the belt was won outright with three consecutive victories by his son "Young Tommy Morris".

The current trophy, the claret jug, was first played for in 1872, when the winner was again Tom Morris Jr. But he was not to know another victory. Three years later, he died of a broken heart after learning of the death of his young wife and child.

► Not all the most sought after pieces of Open Championship memorabilia are old and expensive, although they are often as difficult to obtain as the pieces that are. The "Quiet Please" paddles which marshalls raise as competitors are about to play are usually kept as souvenirs by the marshalls themselves, but just occasionally a few can be persuaded to part with them. This one came from St. Andrews in 1990.

**£10-20**

▼ All Open programmes are highly sought after. The Silvertown Company, which made the Silver King Golf

Balls, gave away this souvenir programme at the 1926 Open Championship at Royal Lytham & St. Anne's. Apart from a description of the club and a plan of the course, the covers and four pages are almost entirely given over to advertisements for the company's balls.

**£70-150**

▲ Postcards are among the most common and evocative Open memorabilia. This one from the Valentine series, *Famous Golfers* shows the eventual winner, Harry Vardon, at the start of the 1903 Open Championship at Prestwick. Tom Morris is on the left, and the 1902 winner, Alex Herd, is on the right.

**£15-30**

▼ In a rare early photograph, Robert Maxwell waits at Muirfield to present the 1896 Open Trophy to Harry Vardon. The photograph is valuable because it is probably the only copy – in those days there was only one official photographer – and also because this was the first of Vardon's six victories.

**£150-250**

◀ This 1924 Handbook from St. Andrews is the oldest known programme from an Open Championship. As such, although it is only two years older than the Royal Lytham & St. Anne's programme (see left), it earned a surprisingly high price at auction in 1991. But the first example of anything important tends to earn an inflated price. If other examples emerge, the price will be lower.

**£3,000-4,000**

◀ The rarest and most important pieces of memorabilia from Open Tournaments are inevitably the trophies and medals. This very early example was won in 1887 by Willie Park Jr, who won the Open again in 1889. One of the greatest players of his generation, he was also a golf architect and designed, amongst others, the Old Course at Sunningdale.

**£11,000-13,000**

▶ Even the *Radio Times* has a value to collectors if the edition has an Open Championship connection. Here the cover for 30 June 1933, shows Gene Sarazen teeing off at Sandwich. Very few copies of the *Radio Times* have survived from this era.

**£15-20**

# Ryder Cup

The greatest of all professional team tournaments is the Ryder Cup, which was founded by an English seed merchant called Samuel Ryder and first played at Worcester, Massachusetts, on 3–4 June 1927.

Ryder, who took up golf for his health only in late middle age, learned to play at the St. Alban's Verulam Golf Club in Hertfordshire and soon became passionately devoted to the game. His tournament, which was held every two years between a team from the United States and a team from Great Britain and Ireland, was at first evenly matched, with the home team winning every time. After the first American win on English soil in 1937, however, the tide turned dramatically. The British and Irish team's win in 1957, under the leadership of Dai Rees, was the only one in the course of the next 42 years.

As a result, in 1979, it was agreed that America's opponents could include professional golfers from the whole of Europe. This move helped to revive waning interest in the competition, and in 1985, led by Tony Jacklin on home soil, the Europeans finally achieved victory. Today the close-fought tournament is one of the most popular in the golfing calendar.

◄ The spectators' pin-on tickets for the 1971 Ryder Cup were made of silk and issued in booklets with a different colour for each day. This complete set is a rare find for a collector, as the valuable tickets have clearly not been used. While not being particularly old, these apparently ordinary items are significant because they exist before the changes in the British team.

**£70-100**

▼ An unusually high-quality photograph from 1931 shows the founder of the competition (on the right) greeting Abe Mitchell before the start of the Ryder Cup at Scioto, Columbus, Ohio.

Mitchell, a member of the first British team, was Ryder's friend and personal coach at the St. Alban's Verulam Club, and he was also the model for the statuette on the top of the cup.

**£30-50**

# RYDER CUP
### OFFICIAL SOUVENIR PROGRAMME

TO BE PLAYED
TUESDAY
AND
WEDNESDAY,
JUNE 29-30,
1937.

ON THE
SOUTHPORT
AND
AINSDALE
COURSE,
SOUTHPORT,
LANCS.

THE SIXTH INTERNATIONAL GOLF MATCH
GREAT BRITAIN versus THE UNITED STATES OF AMERICA
This Official Programme is published by the Professional Golfers' Association and the proceeds will be devoted to the Ryder Cup Fund.

### PRICE ONE SHILLING

▲ Some of the early souvenir programmes were well worth their price, and that value is reflected today in the price that collectors are prepared to pay for them. This one, for the sixth Ryder Cup in 1937, which was also held at Southport, is the same size as the earlier example, but it contains much more. In addition to a plan of the course, a few advertisements and several pages on the pleasures of holidaying in Southport, there are photographs of the previous teams and a grid plan for the foursomes. The 1937 Ryder Cup was also the one at which the Americans won for the first time on British soil. The American team captained by Walter Hagen was victorious over the British team led by Charles Whitcombe, by 8–4.

### £75-150

▶ The souvenir programme for the fourth Ryder Cup, which was held at Southport in Lancashire, measures 9 x 6in (22.8 x 15.2cm). Older and rarer programmes in good condition, such as this one, are inevitably more valuable than most.

### £70-100

◀ The Bakelite badges for the 1971 Ryder Cup at the Old Warson Country Club, St. Louis, were particularly attractive, which may be why so many of them have survived. They were issued to everyone involved in the tournament.

### £20-35 each

## COLLECTING

The popularity of the Ryder Cup is demonstrated by the huge interest it engenders, even among those who are not keen golfers. It is therefore surprising that the variety of items from early tournaments is limited and relatively expensive. Contemporary pieces are widely available, however, and official and souvenir programmes and other publications are easily obtained on both sides of the Atlantic, together with books, videos and other memorabilia.

# RYDER CUP
### OFFICIAL SOUVENIR PROGRAMME

PRICE 1/-

THE FOURTH INTERNATIONAL GOLF MATCH
GREAT BRITAIN versus THE UNITED STATES OF AMERICA
TO BE PLAYED ON THE SOUTHPORT AND AINSDALE COURSE,
SOUTHPORT
ON MONDAY AND TUESDAY, JUNE 26-27, 1933.
This Official Programme is published by the Professional Golfers' Association and the proceeds will be devoted to the British Ryder Cup Fund.

# The Masters

One of the world's greatest professional tournaments, the U.S. Masters, was founded by the world's greatest amateur, Bobby Jones. In 1930 Jones became the only man ever to win the US Amateur Championship and the Open Championships of both the United States and Great Britain in the same year. After that he promptly retired. But in 1934 he came back to take part in his own tournament on the beautiful Augusta National Course in Georgia, where every hole is named after the shrubs and flowers that surround it. Officially known as "The Annual Invitation Tournament", it was always described as "The Masters" by journalists, and in 1938 Jones agreed to change the name.

The record for the most wins in the Masters belongs to Jack Nicklaus, whose sixth win, at the age of 46, also won him the title of "oldest winner". The youngest winner so far is Severiano Ballesteros, who won in 1980 at the age of 23. Until 1988 no British golfer had won the Masters, but since then it has been won by Sandy Lyle, Ian Woosnam, and twice by Nick Faldo.

The Masters has as much of a special place in the hearts of golfing collectors as it does in the hearts of those who follow the game. Many of the items connected with the tournament are highly sought after: the most coveted of these would surely be one of the famous green jackets.

◀ Masters tickets are particularly valuable because they are not available to the general public. Indeed, the whole Augusta course is only open to non-members for six days each year during the tournament. Most of the competition tickets are debentures and are passed between generations within the same family.

**£20-35 each**

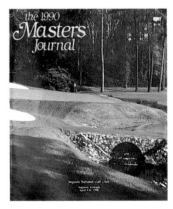

▲ Much less expensive than the early programmes but also widely collected are the lavishly illustrated historical journals that are now brought out with every tournament. Where glossy official tournament programmes cannot be found, this type of publication is of increasing interest to collectors.

**£3-5**

► Official Masters programmes were only issued for the first few tournaments and they are now very rare. Most of those on the market are just unscrupulously convincing copies. This one, however, is the rarest and most valuable of all – a genuine programme from the very first Masters. More recently, Bobby Jones' original spectators' guide and map *(see right)* is now being reproduced in the annual Masters programme.

**£7,000-10,000**

*First*
ANNUAL
INVITATION
TOURNAMENT

*Augusta*
*NATIONAL*
*GOLF*
*CLUB*

MARCH - 22 - 23 - 24 - 25
AUGUSTA GEORGIA

## COLLECTING

It would be unfair to pretend that there is a huge amount of golfing memorabilia relating to the early years of the Masters tournament. This unfortunate situation is deliberate! When the event was originally devised by Bobby Jones, he insisted that advertising was not to be allowed on the course and that the programme should not be more elaborate than a single sheet of paper with the starting order on one side and a map of the course on the other. Indeed, the first Masters Tournament in 1934 was little more than an informal gathering of Jones' old friends, eventually won by Horton Smith. There fore today, apart from rare official items like green jackets or early golf course flags, collectors will find only unofficial publications and small pieces of ephemera, such as tickets and parking passes. However, even small items related to such an important event can be a great addition to a collection.

1986
*Augusta*
*NATIONAL*
*GOLF*
*CLUB*
00228
APRIL 9
WEDNESDAY
PRACTICE
ROUND

PAR-3
CONTEST

TICKET MUST BE DISPLAYED

00228

◄ The only day when the Augusta course is open to the general public is the Wednesday before every Masters championship, when a "Par Three" tournament is held; the tickets for this, although easier to obtain, are still sought after by collectors.

**£12-18**

► Even a parking permit for the Masters has value to a collector. Like the tickets, they are as exclusive as the competition itself and unlike the parking permits from most competitions, they are not so often thrown away.

**£12-18**

№ 5709

MASTERS TOURNAMENT
PATRON
PARKING PERMIT
1982

# *Amateur Championships*

Although the British Open Championship began in 1860, there was no amateur championship until 1885, when the first was held by the Royal Liverpool Golf Club at Hoylake. Less than ten years later, in 1893, a Ladies' Golf Union was formed and the first Ladies' Amateur Championship was held at Portrush, in Northern Ireland, and in 1895, in the same year as the first U.S. Open for men, amateur championships for men and women were held in the United States.

After an abortive start the first tournament of the Walker Cup, named after the president of the U.S.G.A, was played in 1922. Originally intended as a team event for all golfing nations, only the British sent a team in that year, and the event remains the amateur equivalent of the Ryder Cup.

The origins of the women's competition, the Curtis Cup, were established in 1905. After playing in the British Women's Amateur, two American sisters, Harriet and Margaret Curtis offered to put up a trophy for a regular tournament, and in 1932 the first Curtis Cup match was played at Wentworth.

▲ Photographs make another rich record of amateur championships. This one shows Lawson Little with the U.S. Amateur Trophy after winning it for the second time in 1935. Little was the only man to win both the British and American Amateur Championships. He turned professional in 1936, won the Canadian Open in that year, and the U.S. Open in 1940.

**£20-35**

49th AMATEUR CHAMPIONSHIP
U.S.G.A.
OAK HILL COUNTRY CLUB
ROCHESTER, N.Y.
AUGUST 25 - SEPTEMBER 3, 1949
SEASON BADGE
**PRESS**
**509**
GROUNDS ONLY

49th AMATEUR CHAMPIONSHIP
U.S.G.A.
OAK HILL COUNTRY CLUB
ROCHESTER, N.Y.
AUGUST 25 - SEPTEMBER 3, 1949
SEASON BADGE
**GUEST**
Federal Tax $1.67
**641**
GROUNDS & CLUB

◀ ▲ As with the Opens, even the entrance badges to amateur championships are sought after. These, from the U.S. Amateur Championship 1949, are a little more valuable than ordinary admission badges, as they are rarer complimentary passes.

**£15-20 each**

FRIDAY 9th AND SATURDAY 10th JUNE 1972
WESTERN GAILES GOLF CLUB

Price 30p

◄ The women's equivalent of the Walker Cup, the Curtis Cup, was also intended to "stimulate friendly rivalry among the women golfers of many lands" – the inscription that appears on the trophy. But by the time the tournamant was established, the competing nations included only the United States, Great Britain and Ireland. Programmes from the tournament are not difficult to find, and many collectors try to build up whole sequences.

**£20-35**

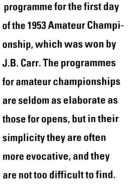

◄ The medals won by amateur champions are among the most valuable items of championship memorabilia. This one, in 22-carat gold, was won in 1933 at the Royal Liverpool Golf Club by the Hon. Michael Scott, who, at the age of 55, was the oldest man ever to win it. He had previously been Australian Amateur Champion four times and Australian Open Champion twice.

**£1,200-2,000**

ENGLISH AMATEUR CHAMPIONSHIP 1955

WON WITH PENFOLD PATENTED GOLF BALL

Further ahead—as usual

▲ Inexpensive advertising posters such as this, issued after the 1955 English Amateur Championship at Royal Lytham & St. Anne's, were usually thrown away when the time came to replace them. But today the survivors are inexpensive pieces of golfing history. This one measures approximately 12 x 20in (30 x 50cm).

**£10-15**

▼ The official programme for the first day of the 1953 Amateur Championship, which was won by J.B. Carr. The programmes for amateur championships are seldom as elaborate as those for opens, but in their simplicity they are often more evocative, and they are not too difficult to find.

**£30-50**

The AMATEUR CHAMPIONSHIP 1953

PLAYED OVER THE LINKS OF THE
Royal Liverpool Golf Club
HOYLAKE
25th — 30th May

OFFICIAL PROGRAMME AND DRAW

MINIMUM 1/- PRICE

TUESDAY

AMATEUR GOLF CHAMPIONSHIP, 1952 — Top Half — THURSDAY, 29th MAY

▲ This unusual and historic item is the draw sheet for the 1952 Amateur Championships with all the scores filled in, giving a complete record of the tournament.

**£8-15**

# Other Major Tournaments

The four most important individual professional tournaments in golf, known as "the Majors", are also the most important to collectors. Beside the oldest, the British Open, and the most recent, the Masters, the other two are the United States Open, first held at Newport, Rhode Island, on 4 October 1895, and the United States P.G.A. Championship, which was first held in the year that the U.S. Professional Golfers' Association was founded, 1916.

There are, however, many other professional tournaments which attract the attention of collectors, such as the World Matchplay Championship, the tournaments on the U.S. and European P.G.A. Tours, the British Ladies' Open and the four Women's Majors in the United States – the Ladies' Open, the L.P.G.A. Championship, the Du Maurier Classic and the Nabisco Dinah Shore. Items from any of these competitions, and also from the "classics" and some of the leading charity events, are always sought after, particularly if they can be associated with one of the leading players.

▲ In the Ladies' Open at the Royal Cinque Ports Golf Club in 1902 every contestant was given a memento book to mark the occasion. This is one of the very rare survivors. Fascinating historic items such as this from the earliest open tournaments are very few and far between.

£300-400

◄ This spectator's plastic badge for the U.S. Open shows that in 1949 an admission pass for the tournament was $7.50. Today it costs over $100. Every year many of the entry tickets and badges to Majors are kept as mementos, and in consequence they are not particularly rare, but they are in such demand with collectors that they are surprisingly expensive.

£18-30

| HOLES | 1 | 2 | 3 | 4 | 5 | 6 | 7 | 8 | 9 | OUT | | 10 | 11 | 12 | 13 | 14 | 15 | 16 | 17 | 18 | IN | TOTAL |
|---|---|---|---|---|---|---|---|---|---|---|---|---|---|---|---|---|---|---|---|---|---|---|
| MY SCORE | | | | | | | | | | | | | | | | | | | | | | |

### OFFICIAL SCORECARD

CONTESTANT  WOOSNAM, IAN

**USF&G Golf Classic**
March 21, 22, 23, 24

DATE  3/24/91

| HOLES | 1 | 2 | 3 | 4 | 5 | 6 | 7 | 8 | 9 | OUT | | 10 | 11 | 12 | 13 | 14 | 15 | 16 | 17 | 18 | IN | TOTAL |
|---|---|---|---|---|---|---|---|---|---|---|---|---|---|---|---|---|---|---|---|---|---|---|
| YARDS | 398 | 519 | 200 | 349 | 463 | 557 | 445 | 176 | 370 | 3477 | | 420 | 550 | 158 | 380 | 469 | 542 | 442 | 207 | 471 | 3639 | 7116 |
| PAR | 4 | 5 | 3 | 4 | 4 | 5 | 4 | 3 | 4 | 36 | | 4 | 5 | 3 | 4 | 4 | 5 | 4 | 3 | 4 | 36 | 72 |
| | 3 | 5 | 2 | 3 | 4 | 5 | 3 | 3 | 4 | 32 | | 4 | 4 | 2 | 4 | 4 | 5 | 4 | 3 | 5 | 35 | 67 |

Scores must be verified and recorded at each hole.
Questions in dispute must be referred to the Rules Committee.

MARKER'S SIGNATURE

On completion of the round, this card shall be
signed by the scorer, verified and signed by the
contestant and handed to scorer's table.

CONTESTANT'S SIGNATURE

▲ Scorecards from classic events are always worth collecting, particularly when they have been used, and are signed by one of the leading players. This one, signed by Ian Woosnam, shows his 67 on a par 72 course in the 1991 U.S.F. and G. Golf Classic.

**£8-15**

▼ Postcard fairs are a rich hunting ground for collectors of championship memorabilia, but as many collectors specialize in all kinds of golfing postcards, there are few bargains to be found. This card is particularly interesting because it shows the great Dorothy Campbell driving off at St. Andrews in the 1908 Ladies Open. In the following year she won both the British and U.S. Championships and by the end of her career she had amassed over 750 prizes.

**£18-25**

(J.PATRICK)
LADIES' OPEN CHAMPIONSHIP, ST.ANDREWS 1908, MISS D.CAMPBELL DRIVING FROM 1ST TEE.

▼ More recent and less expensive than the 1949 spectator's badge *(see left)*, this plastic badge bearing the emblem of the Oakmont Club, a squirrel, was sold simply as a souvenir at the 1983 U.S. Open.

**£2-4**

83rd U.S. OPEN OAKMONT

### THE U.S. OPEN

An unofficial U.S. Open was held at the St. Andrew's Club in Yonkers in 1894 with only four professionals. But the first official tournament was played the following year after the formation of the U.S.G.A. The championship organisers maintain the highest standards of play – today many courses are regarded as simply not difficult enough for the competition.

# Miscellaneous

People have many different reasons and motivations for collecting golf memorabilia. It may simply be pursued for fun; a hobby to which the collector allocates as much time as he or she wishes on a week-to-week basis. There are those interested in the evolution of the game in terms of equipment, competitions and golfing stars. This area of collecting can be costly as pieces of the greatest historical significance are often rare, but the purchase of golfing ephemera, for example, can be a less expensive way of maintaining an accurate record of the game's development. Some people are fond of golf as a decorative feature: this final chapter draws together some disparate areas of collecting that have hitherto gone unmentioned. Textiles, furniture and even children's toys have featured golf as a theme, and these have been snapped up eagerly by those keen to bring the game into their homes. Some people collect anything and everything to do with the game. This will certainly add up to a vast number of objects, but it is often more satisfactory to have an ordered approach to a collection, buying a few, more interesting and better quality pieces. Finally, although it is true that some golfing antiquities, such as old "featheries", are very valuable, the market for collectables can be volatile and so not a place where guaranteed investments can necessarily be made. Those with a genuine interest in the game will not be concerned with whether or not a particular piece will appreciate in value, rather the item is bought for itself and the enjoyment it will bring.

As well as those areas covered so far, golf has influenced all kinds of unusual and interesting products and novelties. Some of these have a very tenuous link with the game, but it is often this eccentricity that makes many of these items so collectable today.

One famous example of sort of piece was sold auction in London in 1983 for £60, and is affectionately known as "The Birdie". This extraordinary lot comprised a glazed oak case containing and displaying a stuffed bird that was unfortunately killed by a golf ball in flight during a game played in around 1915. The bird was mounted inside the case apparently facing the flight of the fatal ball! A further example is a novelty piece by Beatrix Potter. Dating from the end of the last century, sold for £130 in 1979, "Jeremy Fisher at Gleneagles" sat on a green shaped like a lily-pad and held a golf club. These items would not be made for general consumption now, and so are of particular interest to golf collectors.

Games are another important category of golfiana. As golf has always been a fashionable and recreational sport it did not take toy and game manufacturers long to take up the theme and bring it into the home. Games such as "Galloping Golf" and many others involving cards or dice *(see pp.142–143)* have been devised over the past century. Even Jacques & Son, better known as makers of croquet sets, published a game called "St. Andrews" – The New Golfing Game, which they described as "a novel idea for the entertainment of golfers and others … every Golf Club should order this for its members' fun". Golfing toys, made in Britain, the United States and Germany, were also produced in abundance during the first part of the century.

---

*(left, top) A complete set of shirt buttons on a golfing card, United States c.1920; £10–18*
*(left, main) A golfing "hole-in-one" slot machine, United States c.1955; £250–350*
*(above) Rare plastic "Snoopy" ornament, c.1980; £5–10*

# Games & Puzzles

Golfing games and puzzles were available to adults almost a generation before the toy manufacturers began to cater for their children. The first games, introduced around 1900, were aimed at enthusiasts and were intended to give them an alternative when darkness or bad weather precluded the real thing. Many were ingenious miniaturizations and involved putting with little clubs or mechanical figures around obstacles laid out on a carpet or a lawn. The development of these games culminated in Schoenhut's Indoor Golf, which was introduced in the U.S.A. in 1921 by a company that had already become famous for wooden circus animals and musical toys. Each full set consisted of a baize green and tee, four bunkers, balls, spare clubs, score cards and two 5in (12.7cm) figures, known as "Sissy Lofter" and "Tommy Green", who were attached to the ends of full-size club shafts and could be made to swing their own little clubs by means of a trigger mechanism.

By the time Schoenhut's game appeared, the boom in card and board games which followed the First World War had led to a huge increase in the number with golfing themes. While few require any knowledge of golf, their attractive packing alone makes them extremely collectable.

▼ "Golfing", a "quality" game made by Chad Valley at Harborne in England around 1912, was invented by Sir Frederick Frankland Bart. The extremely well moulded and hand-painted lead "flats" were moved along the intricate and eventful course in accordance with the numbers selected by the spin of the top.

**£250-325**

▼ "Tommy Green" and "Sissy Lofter" with balls and two other pieces from a complete set of Schoenhut's Indoor Golf. Complete sets of this sought-after game are very hard to find; most collectors have to buy them piece by piece.

**£500-700**

▼ This "Zag-Zaw" puzzle, with 350 pieces, was the first design in a series of "Royal Picture Play Puzzle Scenes" made by Raphael Tuck & Sons around 1900. Like many of the best old puzzles and calendars, it has been framed, but it has clearly

never been hung in direct sunlight, as the colours are still very bright.

**£90-150**

▼ Dating from around 1910, this hand-cut jigsaw has been signed by the artist, R.R. Jane. Although framing is the best way to display and protect old puzzles, they should never be stuck to the backing board as this will reduce the value.

**£80-150**

◄ This is a rare example of a fine, "one-off", home-made puzzle. The famous Michael Brown painting of the fourth hole at Westward Ho! on the 1913 Life Association of Scotland Calendar has been laid on wood and then hand-cut with a small fretsaw.

**£150-275**

▲ Several of the games which were marketed in the USA at the beginning of the century can still be found at auctions. One is "The Popular Game of Golf", made by Parker Brothers of Salem, Mass. in 1896. The interior of the box is a nine-hole course, and the wooden pieces are kept in a drawer at the side.

**£200-350**

► Another well known and sought after American game is "The Game of Golf", which was made by Clark & Snowdon of New York around 1912. The moves of the wooden playing pieces were directed by the spin of an arrow on a rectangular card.

**£200-350**

# *Toys*

Golfing toys first appeared on the market during the 1920s. By then the game was so popular that Britains and other makers of lead soldiers and farmyard models could see a growing market for lifelike, hand-painted, scale-model golfers among the children of golfing families, and the many manufacturers of tin and mechanical toys began to produce brightly painted golfers with clockwork motors for the same market.

Although there are still many items of golf memorabilia which can form the basis of a collection at very little expense, toys are not among them. Toy collecting is a widespread and well established hobby, and lead models and tin-toy golfers are highly prized not only among golf collectors but also among toy collectors who have no particular interest in the game.

As with all toys, the value increases considerably if the golfing toy retains its box, and indeed the designs and the quality of the lithography on many boxes are so good that they are very attractive and desirable pieces of ephemera in their own right.

▲ Britain's lead figures of golfers in good condition are rare and extremely sought after. Unlike this one, made around 1927, most of the survivors have chipped paintwork and have lost their movable arms.

**£75-135**

▼ Cable-operated golfers such as this used a wire plunger or a puff of air to make the arms swing. They were always hand-painted and were used for table-top or arcade games.

**£60-100**

▼ There is little doubt that the best modern tin toys will rise in value over the years. This Mechanical Bear Golfer, which was made in Japan around 1950 by the Cragstan Company, is already worth many times its original price. When the clockwork mechanism has been wound, the bear chips the ball into the net and then swings back to strike again each time the ball rolls back to his feet. He still retains his brightly lithographed box, which adds to his value, compensating for the drop in value caused by the loss of an ear.

**£100-185**

▼ "Jocko the Golfer" was made in the USA around 1920, probably by Behrend & Rothschild. At the pull of a string in the back of his stand, Jocko swung his club and drove a little golf ball across the carpet. Although he no longer has any of his golf balls, he still has his box, which calls him a "wonder toy".

£295-450

▼ Not a toy, but nevertheless for the nursery, this hand painted fire screen, made around 1955, combined one of the world's most popular games with one of its most popular characters.

£200-325

▼ Several of the best metal toys are being reproduced today in a good enough quality to be collected, particularly as the originals are now so rare and expensive. This "Birdie Putt" money box modelled on a 1920s original, was made in Taiwan. At the push of a button, the caddy lifts the flag as the golfer putts the coin into the hole.

£12-25

▲ Even before the toy manufacturers began to cater for the golfing market, little golfing toys and trinkets were available to enthusiasts in special boxes of Christmas crackers. Surprisingly, this set of a dozen Tom Smith's crackers in their very attractive box have survived unpulled since around 1900.

£85-160

▼ The Chad Valley golfer in his traditional red jacket is even rarer than a Britains model (see left). The casting is much cruder and in this case the paintwork is not in the best condition, but the rarity still makes it valuable.

£90-160

# Buttons & Badges

As golf developed throughout the latter part of the 19th century into a game of social standing and style, so the players themselves began to enjoy decorating their clothes with appropriate accessories. Pieces were already being made for activities such as hunting, shooting and sailing, and it was not long before manufacturers saw the commercial opportunities of the venture.

Golfing jewelry *(see pp. 94–95)* and wrist watches *(see pp. 96–97)* were soon joined by colourfully-enamelled buttons, cuff-links, tie pins and lapel badges. The majority of these pieces were luxury goods made for men and women who were enthusiastic about their game, and keen to show off their interest. Buttons, usually found with golfing figures or crests of golf clubs, were worn on waistcoats, often with matching cuff-links and tie pins. Even sets of dress buttons for evening wear were produced with golfing motifs. These types of accessories remained popular until the 1920s.

Not a fashion accessory but a method of advertising, less expensive enamelled badges have also been made by companies in order to promote their products.

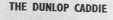

▼ Most unusually, and adding considerably to its value, this Dunlop Caddie pin from the 1920s is still on its card. Pins like these are now being reproduced, so collectors should look at the back to make sure from the date and trade mark that the pin is original.

**£25-40**

▲ The golf club is an ideal shape for a tie pin. This one, in 14-carat gold, was made in the 1930s, but similar pins were made from the 1900s onwards, and they are still being made today. Another popular golfing motif for tie pins, is a single pearl representing a golf ball.

**£100-150**

▼ Like the best cuff-links, the best enamelled dress buttons also had a different picture in each panel. For the modern collector, however, they are better value, even when, like these, they were made as early as 1900. Perhaps because they are now less useful, they usually cost less than the cuff-links.

**£350-500**

▲ Like Dunlop, the Penfold and Bromfield companies also produced badges to advertise their balls in the 1920s. Although, like most, this one no longer has its card, it is still in very good, scratch-free condition. As with the famous Dunlop pin, these are now being reproduced.

**£18-30**

▲ It is very unusual to find any tie clasp made as early as the 1920s, then most gentlemen used pins. It is more unusual to find one as elegant as this one in 14-carat gold and enamel.

**£350-450**

▼ Most of the good quality enamelled cuff-links made in the 1920s and 1930s were 18-carat gold; and the best of them, such as these, had different pictures in each of the four hand-painted panels.

**£600-800**

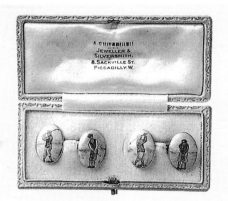

◄ Sometimes the less expensive pieces of jewelry are also the most elegant. These sterling silver cuff-links with the same enamel silhouette on each were made in England in the early 1920s. Fine cuff-links like these, in both silver and gold, are not too difficult to find.

**£150-225**

## COLLECTING

Many golfing accessories on the market today are are found still in their boxes which helps to maintain their value. Although they are by no means rare, sets of buttons, cufflinks and tie pins are as expensive today as they were when they were new, perhaps because they are among the few old items of golfing memorabilia that can still be used, even if only occasionally. Collectors should be aware that similar items are becoming popular again today, and so reproductions are common. Genuine early pieces will be identifiable by their hallmark if made of gold or silver.

Promotional enamelled pins and badges have recently become extremely sought after, and are one of the best ways to build up a golfing collection for those with a limited budget.

# Textiles, Knitwear & Needlepoint

Since before the beginning of the century all fashionable sports have been a constant inspiration to the designers of clothing and textiles, and golf has been no exception. The game has appeared regularly in the motifs on materials for curtains and upholstery. It has been used to provide decorative themes by tailors, shirtmakers, couturiers and haberdashers, more often than not on clothing and accessories that were never intended to be seen on the links. It formed the basis of widely published patterns for needlepoint and knitwear; and today the home-made results of these are as prized by collectors as any other items.

The most famous names in the world of fashion still use golfing themes, and shrewd collectors can often spot the "limited editions" that will be sought after and rise in value in only a few years.

◄ Many of the sweaters and other articles of knitwear which are now prized by collectors were home-made from pattern books such as this one, which was published in 1924. Peace Dale was a mail order company in Madison Avenue, New York, and its 48-page book of men's and women's golf patterns also included three cards wrapped in samples of all the company's yarns, or knitting wools, together with suggestions for colour combinations.

Most unusually, this book is in pristine condition and still has its sample cards, providing the enthusiast with an opportunity to make up a whole range of new 1920s-style golfing sweaters.

**£18-28**

◄ The tapestry on this cushion is in fact modern, although judging by the red jacket and plus fours it looks as though it was stitched 50 or 60 years ago. It was made from a kit, but nevertheless, like all the well-made products of tapestry kits, it acquired additional value on completion.

**£60-90**

► Machine made by Robert Scott of America, this bright golfing pullover is nevertheless already a collector's item, as are many comparatively recent products from famous firms like Pringle and Burberry.

**£28-50**

► This masterly and delicate design was hand-painted on silk around 1934. It has not been signed, and the edges of the silk, measuring 30 x 36in (76 x 91cm), have been hand-rolled, which suggests that it may have been intended as a precious "one-off" scarf.

**£90-170**

► It is unusual to find something as mundane as a tray-cloth in a frame, but this one, printed in the late 1920s or early 30s was clearly highly prized by its owner even when it was new, as it has never been used.

**£50-85**

▼ Like many rare silk scarves today, this one has been framed. It measures 24 x 30in (70 x 76cm) and was printed in the United States between 1898 and 1902. Very few golfing scarves from this period have survived, and this one is unusual not only for its quality but also its condition.

**£600-900**

◄ Another tapestry made from a modern kit, used to cover a footstool. There are a number of kits like this on the market today, and many collectors or just golf enthusiasts who are eager to buy the finished products when they are expertly made. Like the results of earlier knitting kits, they will undoubtedly be among tomorrow's most sought-after memorabilia.

**£70-100**

# *A Miscellany*

The field of golfing memorabilia is almost infinite. There is nothing with a golfing connection that is not of interest to collectors, and there are now very few areas of design which have not been influenced by the game. Within their homes golfers have installed stained-glass windows, furniture, door mouldings and even gates which have incorporated golf clubs and golfers in their designs. Catholic collections include golfing door stoppers, tin trays with golfing decorations and slot machines that dispense golf balls. The order of service from a famous golfer's wedding or funeral can often be one of the treasures of a collection. In fact anything that can be shown to have a connection with golf or golfers will acquire a value. Pieces of furniture, for example, can become collectors' items if there is sufficient provenance to show that they once belonged to a well known club or player. Nothing in golf is disposable. In time everything has a value.

▶ These records were issued by ball manufacturers in the late 1930s and sold through professionals and sports shops. The four records in the series were entitled "The Drive", "The Iron", "Approaching" and "Putting", and each was accompanied by a soft practice ball.

**£25-40**

▲ In the 1920s quite a few sets of dining chairs were specially made for golf clubs and the richer players. Most used the same idea in their design, incorporating clubs and a ball in the back-rest and clubs in the tapestry seat. This walnut example is from a set of six on display at the U.S.G.A. Museum.

**£150-250**

▼ Made to attract the lady golfer around 1900 and now a rare treasure for the golfing collector, these unused hair curlers have ebony handles embellished with silver lady golfers.

These are clearly a standard pair of curlers to which the golfers have been added, but even as early as 1900 many articles were specially made for women, including elaborate silver belt buckles.

**£70-150**

▼ The flask is another widely collected item which is expensive but not particularly rare. Like this leather and plate covered example, which was made by Millner & Sons of Sheffield in the late 19th century, many had embossed golfing scenes on the lower casing, which could usually be taken off and used as a cup.

**£300-500**

▲ A hand-painted plaster figure of a golfing Donald Duck from the 1930s, just over 10in (25cm) in height, can be so sought after that it is more valuable to a collector than the work of a silversmith.

**£300-400**

▲ This mahogany ballot box was made for the Prestwick Golf Club around 1840 and it is by no means the only box of its kind to have come onto the market.

When voting whether or not to accept a new member to their club, the members of the committee could put their hand into the box through the hole and then drop their token into the yes or no drawer without the others seeing which way they had voted.

When the box was brought to a sale room, a letter, addressed to the club secretary and dated 28 July 1868, was found in the "no" drawer.

**£4,000-6,000**

▼ The theme on this oak carver, which was also made in the 1920s, is very similar to that used on the walnut dining chair, but the clubs look a bit more out of place in the traditional 18th century design.

**£175-300**

Golfers – "Yell Fore!"

▲ The registration numbers of cars which make up names or words have been popular for some time and their already astonishing values are multiplied when the word brings them into the sphere of golf. In most cases these British numbers are transferred from one car to another and carried on the road, rather than simply kept for display.

**£9,000-12,000**

# Glossary

**Blade** the head of a metal club

**Bramble pattern** where the surface of a golf ball is covered with small bumps

**Brassie** a wooden-headed golf club with a brass plate fitted to the base

**Bulger** a golf club with a rounded "bulging" head

**Bunker** a sand pit designed to trap golf balls during play, also known as a sand trap

**Cleek** a shallow-faced iron designed to hit the ball low and as far as possible

**Cliche** a copy of a medal

**Driver** the club used to hit the ball from the tee

**E.P.N.S.** electro-plated nickel silver

**Face** the part of the head that comes into contact with the ball

**Feather ball** a leather-covered ball filled with feathers

**Gutta percha** a substance similar to rubber, but harder and less elastic. It can be melted down and remoulded

**Gutty ball** a ball made from strips of gutta percha

**Head** the end of the club used to hit the ball

**Hosel** the lower extension of an iron club shaft to which the head is fitted

**Iron** a metal-faced club, usually steel, with a blade rather than a rounded head

**Jigger** shallow-faced iron for chipping and pitching

**Joint** where the head of the club joins the shaft

**Links** coastal golf courses

**Loft** the angle of slope in a club face

**Lofter** a club designed to hit the ball high into the air

**Long nose** an early club with a long, elegant head

**L.P.G.A.** Ladies' Professional Golf Association

**Mashie** an old club equivalent to a five or six iron

**Mesh pattern** where the surface of a ball is covered with small indentations

**Niblick** a small-faced iron with a hickory shaft

**Par** a given number of shots in which a player should complete a particular hole

**P.G.A.** Professional Golfers' Association

**Putter** the club used to hole the ball, usually on or near the green

**R. & A.** Royal and Ancient Golf Club, St. Andrews

**Rubber core ball** a golf ball with a centre composed of elastic thread wound around itself under tension

**Shaft** the handle of the golf club

**Socket** where the shaft of a wooden club joins the head

**Sole** the part of the head that rests on the ground

**Splicing** where the shaft is cut to a tapering point 4½–6in (11.5–15.25cm) to fit into the club head; this was glued and secured with pitched twine or whipping

**Spoon** an old fairway wooden club, equivalent to a three wood

**Stein** a German-style tankard, usually used for drinking beer

**Sweet spot** the point at which the ball hits the face most effectively

**Tee** the point at which the drive is taken on each hole; the peg on which the ball is placed for the tee shot

**Toe** the part of the clubhead farthest from the shaft

**Track iron** a club designed for playing out of cart tracks and hoof marks

**Transitional** a club shape in between long-nose and bulger

**Tyg** a three-handled mug

**U.S.G.A.** United States Golf Association

**Whipping** the binding at the base of the shaft

**Whippy** a word used to describe the flexibility of the shaft of a club

**Wood** a wooden-headed club used for long shots, now also made of metals such as aluminium

### Bibliography and Suggested Reading

Elliot, Allan and May, John Allan *Illustrated History of Golf*
Henderson, Ian and Sturk, David *Golf in the Making*
Hobbs, Michael and Baddiel, Sarah Fabian *Golf: A Visual History*
Olman, John M. and Morton W. *Encyclopedia of Golf*
Olman, Morton W. *Olman's Guide to Golf Antiques and Other Treasures of the Game*
Sprung, Shirley and Jerry *Decorative Golf Collectables*

# Collectable Books

*This list extends the section of the book dealing with collectable golf books. Prices quoted are within a range which compares the value of first editions in very good condition, with later editions.*

Adams, Herbert *Golf House Murder*, 1933 [£20–35]

Alley, Peter *Play the Best Courses: Golf Courses in the British Isles*, 1973 [£15–30]

Baddiel, Sarah Fabian *Golf, The Golden Years*, 1990 [£8–10] *Golfing Ephemera*, 1991 [£6–8] *The World of Golf Collectables*, 1992 [£7–9]

Browning, Robert *History of Golf*, 1955 [£30–70] *Stymie*, 1910 [£75–150]

Campbell, Sir Guy *Golf at Prince's and Deal*, 1950 [£30–70]

Chambers, Charles *Golfing: A Handbook to the Royal and Ancient Game*, 1887 [£150–350]

Clark, Robert *Golf, A Royal and Ancient Game*, 1875 [£300–450]

Cochran, Alistair and Stobbs, John *Search for the Perfect Golf Swing*, 1968 [£18–38]

Collect, Glenna *Ladies in the Rough*, 1928 [£22–45]

Colt, Harry S. *Some Essays on Golf Course Architecture*, first edition, 1920 [£200–400]; reprinted in 1980 [£50–80]

Colville, George M. *Five Open Champions and the Musselburgh Golf Story*, 1980 [£40–65], limited edition with score cards signed by Tom Watson and A. Goaki, leather bound [£85–140]

Cornish, G. and Whitten, R.W. *The Golf Course*, 1981 [£25–40]

Cotton, Henry *Golf, A Pictorial History*, 1975 [£12–18] *Guide to Golf in the British Isles*, 1961 [£15–25] *Hints on Play with Steel Shafts*, 1934 [£45–75] *Picture of the Golf Game*, 1965 [£10–15]

Cotton, Henry and White, Jack *Golfing in Scotland at 100 Holiday Resorts*, 1936 [£15–40]

Cox, Charles *Spalding's Official Golf Guide*, 1897–1942 annually, usually in paper wraps [£10–50]

Currente, Calamo *Half Hours with an Old Golfer*, 1895 [£140–300]

Darwin, Bernard *A Friendly Round*, 1922 [£120–250] *Golf, Pleasures of Life Series*, 1954 [£45–80] *Golf Courses of the British Isles*, 1910 [£150–250] *Golf from The Times*, 1912 [£175–300] *Golfers Gallery of Old Masters* (bound in art prints on card), 1920 [£250–400] *Green Memories*, 1928 [£85–150] *History of Golf in Britain*, 1952 [£60–100] *James Braid*, 1952 [£15–30] *Out of the Rough*, 1932 [£20–40] *Round of Golf on the London and North Eastern Railway*, 1924, three different editions [£100–200] *Tee Shots and Others*, 1911 [£160–220] *Hints on Golf with Supplement on Golfing Outfits* (by Burberry), 1912 (very scarce) [£200–350]

Dobereiner, Peter *Glorious World of Golf*, 1973 [£20–30] *Down the Nineteenth Fairway*, 1983 [£10–15]

Duncan, George *Golf for Women*, 1907 [£30–50]

Evans, Chick *Chick Evans' Golf Book*, 1921 [£20–30]

Evans, Webster *Encyclopedia of Golf*, 1971 [£8–12] *In Praise of Golf*, 1950 [£6–12]

Everard, H.S.C. *History of the Royal and Ancient Golf Club St. Andrews, 1754–1900*, 1907 [£275–400]

Farrar, Guy *Royal Liverpool Golf Club 1869–1932*, 1933 [£10–200]

Forrest, James *Basis of the Golf Swing*, 1925 [£15–30]

Frome, David *Murder on the Sixth Hole*, 1931 [£10–18]

Galico, Paul *Golf is a Friendly Game*, 1942 [£18–30]

Gaul, W.K. *Practical Greenkeeping*, 1913 [£10–20]

Golfer, A. (pseudonym of G. Robb), *Historical Gossip about Golf and Golfers*, 1863 [£1200–1800]

Hagen, Walter *The Walter Hagen Story*, 1956 [£20–30]

Hall Holworthy *Dormie One and other Golf Stories*, 1971 [£65–110]

Harris, Robert, *Sixty Years of Golf*, 1953 [£30–50]

Haultain, Arnold *Mystery of Golf*, 1908 [£40–70]

Hecker, Genevieve *Golf for Women*, 1902 [£80–140]

Helme, Eleanor E. *After the Ball*, 1925 [£15–30] *Lady Golfers' Tip Book* [£10–25]

Henderson, Ian and Shirk, David *Golf in the Making*, 1979 [£40–80] *Shortspoon: F.P. Hopkins, Golf Artist*, 1983 [£60–100]

Herd, Alexander *My Golfing Life*, 1923 [£40–80]

Hezlet, May *Ladies Golf*, 1904 [£60–110]

Hill, J.C.H. *Lyre on the Links and Other Verses*, 1935 [£20–40]

Hillinthorn, Gerald *Your First Game of Golf*, 1891 [£200–400]

Hilton, H.H. *My Golfing Remembrances*, 1907 [£100–150]

Hilton, H.H. and Smith, G.C. *Royal and Ancient Game of Golf* (limited to 900 copies), 1912 [£300–500]; special limited edition of 100 copies [£1000–2000]

Hopkinson, Cecil *Collecting Golf Books 1743-1938*, 1938 [£150–300]; reprint by Grant Books, 1980 [£40–80]

Houghton, George *Addict's Guide to British Golf*, 1959 [£6–10] *Golf Among the Irish*, 1965 [£8–10] *Golf Addict Invades Wales*, 1969 [£8–10] *Golf with a Whippy Shaft*, 1971 [£20–30] *Portrait of a Golf Addict*, 1960 [£6–8]

George Houghton wrote and illustrated all his books which are very humorous. One should collect first editions in wrappers which should not be too difficult. Just a selection of titles listed above

Hughes, W.E. *Chronicles of the Blackheath Golfers*, 1897 [£400–600]

Hunter, Robert *The Links*, 1926 [£70–150]

Hutchinson, Horace *British Golf Links*, 1897 [£225–350] *Fifty Years of Golf*, 1919 [£70–150] *Golf Green and Greenkeeping*, 1906 [£80–200] *Golfing Pilgrim on Many Links*, 1898 [£100–200] *Hints on the Game of Golf*, 1866 (and thirteen further editions) [£25–200] ed. *Famous Golf Links*, 1891 [£80–175] *Book of Golf and Golfers*, 1899 [£80–150] *Golf: The Badminton Library* [£70–140]

Ito, Cho *Golf Treasures*, 1925 [£150–275]

J.A.C.K. (J. McCullough) *Golf in the Year 2000*, 1892 [£100–£225]

Jones, Robert Tyre Jr. *Bobby Jones on Golf*, 1930 [£12–25] *Golf is My Game*, 1960 [£10–18] *Rights and Wrongs*, 1936 [£18–30]

Jones, R.T. and Keeler, O.B. *Down the Fairway*, 1927 [£15–35]; limited edition signed and in a slipcase [£200–300]

Jones, Robert Trent *Golf Course Architecture*, 1936 [£70–150]

Keeler, O.B. *Boy's Life of Bobby Jones*, 1931 [£35–60] *Autobiography of an Average Golfer*, 1925 [£30–55]

Kennard, Mrs Edward *Golf Lunatic and His Cycling Wife*, 1902 [£90–170]

Kerr, John *Golf Book of East Lothian*, 1896 [£200–350]

Kirkaldy, Andrew *Fifty Years of Golf*, 1921 [£60–100]

Leach, Henry *Great Golfers in the Making*, 1907 [£50–90] *Happy Golfer*, 1914 [£40–80] *Letters to a Modern Golfer to his Grandfather*, 1910 [£50–90] *Spirit of the Links*, 1907 [£50–100]

Lee, James P. *Golf in America*, 1895 [£150–300]

Leigh, Dell *Golf at its Best on the L.M.S.*, 1925 [£80–120]

Leigh Bennett, E.P. *Errant Golfer*, 1929 [£20–35] *Some Friendly Fairway*, 1930 [£22–40] *Southern Golf* (Golf in the South), 1935 [£20–35]

Leich, Cecil *Golf*, 1922 [£20–35] *Golf for Girls*, 1911 [£25–40] *Golf Simplified*, 1924 [£18–30]

Longhurst, Henry *Golf Mixture*, 1952 [£12–20] *It Was Good While it Lasted*, 1941 [£10–18] *Never on Weekdays*, 1968 [£12–20] *Only on Sundays*, 1964 [£12–20] *Round in Sixty-eight*, 1953 [£10–18] *Talking About Golf*, 1966 [£8–15]

Locker, Samuel J. *On the Green, An Anthology*, 1922 [£20–35]

Low, John *F.G. Tait: A Record*, 1910 [£40–70]

Low, J. *et al, Nisbet's Golf Year Book*, 1905–1914 [£60–120]

Low, J. and Hilton, H.H. *Concerning Golf*, 1903 [£20–50]

MacDonald, Charles Blair *Scotland's Gift: Golf Reminiscences 1872-1927*, 1928 [£90–150]; limited signed edition of 260 [£250–400]

MacKenzie, Alister *Golf Architecture*, 1920 [£120–250]

MacKern, Mrs L. *Our Lady of the Green*, 1899 [£120–200]

Marietta Six *Golfing Stories*, 1905 [£45–90]

Martin, H.B. *Fifty Years of American Golf*, 1936 [£80–150] Golf Yarns, 1913 [£40–80] *Great Golfers in the Making*, 1932 [£35–75]

Martin, John Stuart *Curious History of the Golf Ball*, 1968 [£70–150]; limited edition, 1968 [£150–225]

McPherson, Rev J.G. *Golf and Golfers Past and Present*, 1891 [£10–250]

Miller, Rev T.D. *Famous Scottish Links*, 1911 [£100–250] *History of Royal Perth Golfing Society*, 1935 [£75–150]

Murdoch, Joseph S.F. *Library of Golf 1743-1966: A Bibliography of Golf Books*, 1968 [£125–200] *Library of Golf Update Booklet*, 1978 [£50–80]

Nash, G.C. *Letters to the Secretary of a Golf Club*, 1935 [£18–30] *General Forcurscue and Co: More Letters*, 1936 [£18-30] *Whelks Post Bag: Still More Letters*, 1937 [£18–30]

Nicklaus, Jack and Wind, H. Warren *The Greatest Game of All*, 1969 [£10–15]

Ouimet, Francis *Game of Golf*, 1932 [£20–40] *Golf Antiques and Other Treasures of the Game*, 1992 [£15–20]

Park, Willie *Art of Putting*, 1920 [£70–120] *The Game of Golf*, 1896 [£80–150]

Peter, H.T. *Reminiscences of Golf and Golfers*, 1890 [£100–180]

Price, Charles *The American Golfer*, 1964 [£15–30] *World of Golf*, 1962 [£12–20]

Punch Magazine *Funny Side of Golf*, 1909 [£40–90]

Ralston, W. *North Again, Golfing This Time*, 1894 [£30–80]

Ray, Edward *Golf Clubs and How to Use Them*, 1922 [£12–20]

Reid, Wm. F.J.I. *Golfing Reminiscences 1887-1925*, 1925 [£80–120]

Reynolds, Frank *Frank Reynolds Golf Book*, 1932 [£75–150] *Hamish McDuff*, 1937 [£60–120]

Robinson, W. *Heath Humours of Golf*, 1923 [£100–200]

Salmond, Dr. J.B. *Story of the R. & A.*, 1956 [£15–30]

Sapper, Uncle James *Golf Match*, 1950 [£30–50]

Sarazen, Gene and Warren Wind, H. *Thirty Years of Championship Golf: The Life Times of Gene Sarazen*, 1950 [£20–50]

Schrite, J.E. *Divots for Dubs*, 1934 [£20–40]

Schultz, Charles M. *Snoopy's Grand Slam*, 1972 [£10–18]

Sherman, James W. J*ocy Gets the Golf Bug*, 1961 [£10–18]

Simpson, Harold *Seven Stages of Golf*, 1909 [£120–250]

Simpson, S.R. *A Green Crop*, 1937 [£40–80]

Simpson, Sir Walter G. *The Art of Golf*, 1887 [£200–350]

Smith, Charles *The Aberdeen Golfers*, 1909 [£150–300]

Smith, G.C. *Side Lights on Golf*, 1907 [£70–150] *World of Golf Isthmian Library* 1898 [£60–120]

Stancliffe *An Astounding Golf Match*, 1914 [£60–90] *The Autobiography of a Caddy Bag*, 1924 [£40–80] *Quick Cuts to Good Golf*, 1920 [£12–18]

Stiley, Louis T. *Fresh Fairways*, 1949 [£12–20] *Green Fairways*, 1947 [£12–20] *The Woman Golfer*, 1952 [£8–14]

Stewart, James Lindsay *Golfiana Miscellanea*, 1887 [£120–180]

Stobart, M.A. *Won at the Last Hole*, 1893 [£35–60]

Stringer, Mabel E. *Golfing Reminiscences*, 1924 [£30–70]

Sutphen, W.G. van T. *The Golfers Alphabet*, 1898 [£80–240] *Golficide and Other Tales*, 1898 [£80–180] *Nineteenth Hole*, 1901 [£75–150]

Sutton, M. *et al, Golf Courses, Design Construction and Upkeep*, 1933 [£120–200]

Sutton, M.H.F. *Layout and Upkeep of Golf Courses and Putting Greens* 1906 [£100–250] *et al, Book of the Links*, 1912 [£120–250]

Taylor, Bert Leston *Line O'Gowf or Two*, 1923 [£25–50]

Taylor, J.H. *Golf, My Life's Work*, 1943 [£30–70] *Taylor on Golf*, 1902 [£30–70]

Taylor, Joshua *The Art of Golf*, 1913 [£25–50] *The Lure of the Links*, 1920 [£20–45]

Thomas, George C. *Golf Architecture in America*, 1927 [£120–200]

Thomson, John *Golfing & Other Poems & Sons*, 1893 [£120–200]

Tinninghurst, A. *Cobble Valley Golf Yarns*, 1915 [£75–180] *The Milt and Other Golf Yarns*, 1925 [£80–180]

Tuloch, W.W. *Life of Tom Morris*, 1908 [£200–400]

Van Dengel, Steven J.H. *Early Golf*, 1982 [£12–25]

Vardon, Harry *My Golfing Life*, 1933 [£60–150] *Progressive Golf*, 1920 [£20–40]

Watson, A. Campbell *Podson's Golfing Year*, 1930 [£20–35]

Webing, W. Hastings *Fore: Call of the Links*, 1909 [£25–45] *Locker Room Ballards*, 1925 [£25–40] *On and Off the Links*, 1921 [£30–50]

Wendehack, Clifford C. *Golf and Country Clubs*, 1929 [£75–200]

Wesson, Doug J. Bertram, *I'll Never Be Cured and Don't Much Care*, 1928 [£20–35]

Wethered, H.N. and Simpson, T. *The Architectural Side of Golf*, 1929 [£120–250]; limited signed edition of 50 copies [£850–1000]

Wethered, Roger *Golf from Two Sides*, 1922 [£18–30]

Wheatley, Vera *Mixed Foursomes*, 1922 [£25–40]

Wind, Herbert Warren *The Story of American Golf*, 1948 [£40–80]

Wodehouse, P.G. *Divots*, 1927 [£20–40] *Golf Omnibus*, 1973 [£15–30] *Heart of a Fool*, 1926 [£15–50] *Clicking of Cuthbert*, 1922 [£20–60] *Wodehouse on Golf*, 1940 [£15–30]

Wood, Harry B. *Golfing Curios and the Like*, 1910 [£150–300]; signed limited edition of 150 copies [£400–1000]

Wright, Harry *Short History of Golf in Mexico*, 1938 [£70–150]

Zahanas, Mildred "Babe" *This Life I've Led*, 1956 [£8–15]

# Buy & Sell

## AUCTION HOUSES

**Christies**
164–166 Bath Street
Glasgow
Scotland
G2 4TG
Tel: 041 332 8134
*Contact:* Edward Monagle
*Sales held:* July

**Phillips**
New House
150 Christledon Road
Chester
CH3 5TD
Tel: 0244 313936
*Contact:* Bob Gowland
*Sales held:* January and July
(small sales held April and
October)

**Sotheby's**
34/35 New Bond Street
London
W1A 2AA
Tel: 071 408 5205
*Contact:* Jon Baddeley
*Sales held:* July

**Bonhams**
Montpelier Galleries
Montpelier Street
London
SW7 1HH
Tel: 071 584 9161
*Contact:* Duncan Chilcott
*Sales held:* March

**Sporting Antiquities**
PO Box 1386
47 Leonard Road
Melrose
Mass. 02176
USA
Tel: 617 662 6588
*Contact:* Kevin McGrath
*Sales held:* May

## DEALERS

**Sarah Fabian Baddiel**
Golfiana
Grays-in-the-Mews
Davies Mews
London
Tel: 071 408 1239
081 452 7243 *

**Rhod McEwan**
Glen Garden
Ballater
Aberdeenshire
Scotland
AB35 5UB
Tel: 0339 755429

**David Neech** *
Golf Interest
PO Box 1226
Eastbourne
BN20 9DH
Tel: 0323 422075

**Manfred Schotten**
The Crypt
109 High Street
Burford
OX18 4RG
Tel: 0993 82 2302

**Bob Pringle**
Old Troon Sporting Antiques
49 Ayr Street
Troon
Ayreshire
Scotland
KA10 6EB
Tel: 0292 311822

**David Brown**
Old St. Andrews' Gallery
10 Golf Place
St. Andrews'
Scotland
KY16 9JA
Tel: 0334 77840

**Col. J.C. Furniss** *
Crossway House
Torthorwald
Dumfries
DG1 3PT
Tel: 0387 75 624
Books only

**Leo Kelly**
6244 Beechwood Road
Matteson
Ill. 60443
USA
Tel: 708 720 0046

**Old Golf Shop** *
325 5th Street
Cincinnati
Ohio 45202
USA
Tel: 513 241 7797

**Richard Donavan** *
PO Box 7070
305 Massachusetts Avenue
Endicott
NY 13760
USA
Tel: 607 785 5874
Books only

**Golf Collectors' Society**
PO Box 20546
Dayton
Ohio 45420
USA
Tel: 513 256 2474

**Greg and Barbara Hall**
24717 East Oakland Road
Bay Village
Ohio 44140
USA
Tel: 216 871 9319

* *Viewing by appointment*

## MUSEUMS

**Ralph W. Miller Golf Library**
**and Museum**
PO Box 3287
1 Industry Hills Parkway
City of Industry
CA 91744
USA
Tel: 818 854 2354

**P.G.A./World Golf Hall of Fame**
PO Box 1908
PGA Boulevard
Pinehurst
North Carolina 28374
USA
Tel: 919 265 6651

**U.S.G.A. Museum and Library**
Golf House
PO Box 708
Liberty Corner Road
Far Hills
NJ 0791
USA
Tel: 908 234 2300

**British Columbia Golf House**
2545 Blanca Street
Vancouver
V6R 4N1
Canada
Tel: 604 222 4653

**British Golf Museum**
Bruce Embankment
St. Andrews
Scotland
KY16 9AB
Tel: 0334 78880

**Heritage of Golf**
Gullane Golf Club
East Lothian
Scotland
EH31 2BB
Tel: 087 57277

# Index

# *Acknowledgements*

8 tSFB, cSM 9 SM 10 tlSM, trSL, bCS 11 tlSM, trIB/AW, blSL, brSL 12 all SM 13 clSM, blSC, brSM 14 all IB/AW 15 tlSM, clSFB crSFB, trSFB, bSFB 16 tSM, cSL, bSM 17 tIB/AW blSL, clSL, crSM, brSL 18 tSM, cSL, bSM 19 tlSM, trSL, blSC, bcSL, brSL 20 allIB/AW 21 all IB/AW 22 allIB/AW 23 all IB/AW 24 all IB/AW 25 tlIB/AW, tcIB/AW, trSL, blIB/AW, bcIB/AW, brSL 26 all SL 27 tlIB/AW, trIB/AW, blSL, brSL 28 tSC, ctSM, cbSM, bSC 29 tSM, ctSM, cbSL, bSL 30 tPNW, ctCM, cbPNW, bPNW 31 tlCM, trPNW, cCM, bSL 32 tSFB, cPS, bPS 33 tlSFB, trPS, blSFB, brSFB 34 tIB/SL, bSFB 35 tlIB/SL, trIB/SL, cSFB, bSA 36 tCS, bSC 37 tlSC, ctIB/SL, cbSC, blSL, bcSM, brSL 38 c, IB/AW, bIB/SL 39 trIB/AW, clIB/SL, blIB/AW, brIB/SL 40 tSFB, bCM 41 all IB/AW 42 tPNW, blPNW, brSFB 43 tlSC, cPNW, blSL, bcPNW, brPNW 44 tBWC, bSFB 45 tlSFB, trIB/SL, clSFB, blIB/SFB, brSFB additional pictures for equipment chapter IB/BWC 46 all SFB 47 SFB 48 tPS, bIB/SL 49 tlSMh, trSL, cIB/SL, blO, brIB/SL 50 tlIB/SL, trIB/SL, cIB/SL, bcIB/SL 51 tcIB/SL, blIB/SL, brPNY 52 all SFB 53 all SFB 54 all SFB 55 all SFB 56 all SFB 57 tlIB/SFB, trSFB, clSFB, crSFB, blSFB, brSFB 58 all SFB 59 all SFB 60 all SFB 61 all SFB 62 all SFB 63 all SFB 64 all SFB 65 all SFB 66 all SFB 67 all SFB 68 all SFB 69 tlIB/SL, trSFB, cSFB, blSFB, brSFB 70 all IB/SFB 71 all IB/SFB 72 tIB/SFB, cSFB, bIB/SFB 73 all IB/SFB 74 all SFB 75 all SFB 76 all SFB 77 all SFB 78 all SFB 79 SFB 80 tlIB/SL, blPNY, brIB/SL 81 tlSA, trSA, cIB/SL, blPNW 82 all SFB 83 all SFB 84 tIB/SL, bSFB 85 tlIB/SFB, trSFB, blIB/SL, brIB/SL 86 all SFB 87 tSFB, clPNW, crSFB, blSFB, brSFB 88 tSFB, cSFB, bIB/SL 89 tlIB/SL, trSFB, clIB/SL, crSFB, bIB/SL 90 tlSFB, cSFB, bPS 91 tlSFB, trPS, clCS, crCS, bSFB 92 all SFB 93 all SFB 94 all SFB 95 all SFB 96 tCS, bCS 97 tSL, clCS, crSFB, bPS 98 tSFB, cBWC 99 SFB 100 all SFB 101 tlPNW, trSFB, clSFB, blSFB, brSFB 102 tIB/SFB, bSFB 103 tlSFB, trSFB, cIB/SL, blSFB, brSFB 104 tSC, cSC, bSFB 105 tlIB/SL, trSFB, cCS, blSL, brSM 106 all SFB 107 all SFB 108 tSFB, bIB/SL 109 tSFB, cPNW, bPNY 110 tCS, bSFB 111 tlSL, cSFB, blSC, brSFB 112 tPNW, bSC 113 tSG, clSG, crSG, bSM 114 all SFB 115 SM 116 tSL, bIB/SL 117 tlPS, trIB/SL, clCS, crCL, bSL 118 tSL, bIB/SL 119 trIB/SL, clIB/SL, blSFB, brPS 120 all SFB 121 tlIB/SL, trIB/SFB, cIB/SFB, blIB/SL, brIB/SL 122 tSFB, cIB/SL, bSFB 123 tlIB/SL, trSFB, cSFB, blSFB, brIB/SL 124 tIB/SL, bSFB 125 tlSFB, trSFB, cSFB, blIB/SL, brIB/SL 126 tPNW, bPS 127 tlPS, trSFB, cIB/SL, blPNW 128 all SFB 129 SM 130 all SFB 131 tlIB/SFB, trSFB, clPNW, crPNW, blSFB, brPNW 132 tIB/SFB, bSFB 133 trSFB, tlIB/SFB, brSFB 134 all SFB 135 tSA, cSFB, bSFB 136 all SFB 137 tlSFB, trPNW, cIB/SFB, blIB/SFB, bSFB 138 tIB/SL, bSFB 139 tlIB/SFB, crSFB, blIB/SFB 140 tSFB, cIB/SL 141 SFB 142 tSFB, bSG 143 tlIB/SFB, trIB/SFB, clIB/SFB, crIB/SL, bIB/SL 144 all SFB 145 tlIB/SL, trSFB, cIB/SFB, blIB/SL, brSFB 146 tPNW, cSFB, bSM 147 tlSFB, trPNW, cSA, bSA 148 tSFB, bIB/SFB 149 tlIB/SFB, trSFB, cSFB, blIB/SFB, brSFB 150 tSFB, cIB/SFB, bSFB 151 tlSM, trSFB, cSM, blSFB, brSC

### Key

| | |
|---|---|
| SFB | photographs provided by Sarah Fabian Baddiel |
| IB/SL | from Sotheby's London, photography by Ian Booth for RCB |
| IB/SFB | from Sarah Fabian Baddiel, photography by Ian Booth for RCB |
| IB/AW | from Alick Watt's collection, photography by Ian Booth for RCB |
| IB/BWC | from Bonhams West Country, photography by Ian Booth for RCB |

*Locations specified refer to place of sale*

| | |
|---|---|
| SM | Sotheby's Musselburg |
| SC | Sotheby's Chester |
| SL | Sotheby's London |
| SG | Sotheby's Glasgow |
| CL | Christie's London |
| CM | Christie's Musselburg |
| CS | Christie's Scotland |
| PNW | Phillips North West |
| PNY | Phillips New York |
| SA | Sporting Antiquities |
| O | Oliver's |